ITALIAN MADE EASY LEVEL 1

*An Easy Step-By-Step Approach to Learn Italian for Beginners
(Textbook + Workbook Included)*

Lingo Mastery

Contents

Preface/About the Language

Italian is the product of the long evolution of the Latin language as well as the many historical and political changes the country faced throughout the centuries. This Romance language is spoken by 66 million people in the world, most of them located in Italy.

However, Italian is also spoken in the Republic of San Marino, Switzerland, Vatican City, the Sovereign Military Order of Malta, and as a minority language in some small areas of Slovenia, Croatia and Brazil.

Each one of Italy's twenty regions has its own dialect, which was influenced by the several waves of invasions in the different areas. Even though dialects are still spoken all over Italy, nowadays it is more common to hear them in the little villages or spoken by the older generations.

Italian is recognized all over the world, thanks to its influence on art, culture, and food. Many Italian words are commonly used in other languages; most of them are related to food or a particular way of living. *Pizza, gelato, fettuccine, paparazzi, dolce vita, ballerina* and even *opera* are among the ones used the most.

Italians are well known for their passion; the way they communicate can't be limited to words. Italian people often use their hands to highlight a concept or to express their feelings. One simple gesture of the hand can often sum up an entire sentence!

With this book, we will learn to master this wonderful language and to appreciate Italian culture.

Structure

Learning a language should be a fun and rewarding experience. The aim of this book is to offer you a self-taught course of study that will allow you to understand the language's grammar as well as the culture it comes from.

This book will provide you with the linguistic, cultural and strategic tools to communicate in Italian. Besides speaking and oral comprehension, we will also consider grammar, phonetics and spelling. The educational progression has been carefully planned so that the student can personalize their experience while practicing the language, using relevant situations.

Each chapter is dedicated to a particular situation the student might find themself in while exploring a new culture. We will talk about family, work, and sport, without forgetting food and fashion of course!

The exercises following each session are designed to reinforce what has been learned while expanding the student's vocabulary. They also aim to enhance the student's confidence and motivation during the learning process.

We hope you are ready to learn this amazing language in a fun and relaxed way!

Iniziamo! (Let's start!)

Introduction

Far from being an exhaustive guide to the Italian language, this book is intended to give you the tools you need to start communicating in Italian right away. Take your time exploring the different sections—do not rush through them, but rather **enjoy this journey** into the Italian language.

Our objective at this initial level is to develop basic communication and interaction skills, by providing the reader with oral and written exercises of low and medium complexity. It will prepare the student to interact in Italian in everyday situations and in different contexts. This book covers level A1 in the Common European Framework of Reference for Languages (CEFR).

This book is ideal for people who are learning Italian on their own or in a classroom setting. It is also a valuable companion for a trip overseas, or a safety blanket before an important meeting with an Italian company. Whether you are trying to learn Italian for pleasure or for business, we would like to make your life easier and less stressful.

Try completing all the exercises as they are structured. That way, you will not only practice what you are learning in that given section, but also consolidate your learning of words and rules throughout the whole book.

At the end of each chapter, we included a section with some of the most common sayings in Italian. They will not only enrich your vocabulary and give you a chance to speak like a native, but also provide you with insight into Italian culture.

If anything, **learn from the Italians:** go with the flow, enjoy the simple things, and take a break whenever you feel overwhelmed!

Recommendations

This book is a tool for anyone who is motivated to learn Italian. Let us give you some useful recommendations and tips:

- **Mistakes happen:** We all make mistakes, especially when learning a new language, but that should not discourage us; on the contrary, it should encourage us to learn from them. People will appreciate your efforts!

- Sometimes, when learning a new language, one might get frustrated when trying to communicate because of a lack of vocabulary. **Never give up!** Try to explain the concept using alternatives for the word you don't remember. It is a good exercise for your brain!

- Italian is a phonetic language, so pronunciation is very **easy**: Italian is read as it is written; i.e., words are spelled as they are pronounced. Once you learn some basic sounds, you will be all set!

- You do not need to rush, as each person has their own pace. **Take your time**; you will learn everything.

- The best way to learn a new language is to **immerse yourself** in that culture. Many Italian newspapers can be found online; try to read a simple article, or even just some ads. See if you can find some of the words you learned during your lessons. Podcasts are also a wonderful and fun way to refine your pronunciation and develop an ear for Italian.

- Last, but not least, **practice makes perfect!**

HOW TO GET THE AUDIO FILES

Some of the excercises throughout this book comes with accompanying audio files.

You can download these audio files if you head over to
www.LingoMastery.com/italian-me1-audio

SECTION 1

SECTION 1 - BASI
FOUNDATIONS

ALFABETO E PRONUNCIA
THE ALPHABET AND ITS PRONUNCIATION

The Italian alphabet consists of 21 letters (*lettere*): 16 consonants (*consonanti)* and 5 vowels (*vocali*).

Many letters, especially the vowels **e** and **o**, can have slightly different sounds based on the letters that follow. For our purposes, approaching Italian for the first time and building up confidence to have a conversation, the alternative sounds are not really important. They are slight variations, often not perceived even by Italian natives. Make your life easier and learn the following sounds. There will be no surprises; Italian is read as it is written, which also means that words are spelled as they are pronounced.

In the following table you will find the **pronunciation of the letters of the Italian alphabet**. Start practicing by reading the word examples next to each letter.

This way you can get familiar with the sounds and start memorizing some simple words!

Letter	Name	Pronunciation	As in...
A	A (*ah*)	[ʌ]	**Albero** *tree*
B	Bi (*be*)	[b]	**Bambino** *boy*
C	Ci (*chi*)	/tʃi/ [c *before e, i*] /k/ [k *before a, o, u*]	**Cielo** *sky* **Cane** *dog*
D	Di (*de*)	[d]	**Dito** *finger*
E	E (*ai*)	[e]	**Elefante** *elephant*
F	Effe (*eh-feh*)	[f]	**Fiore** *flower*
G	Gi (*ge*)	/g/ [g *before a, o, u*] /dʒ/ [g *before i, e*]	**Gatto** *cat* **Gonna** *skirt* **Gelato** *ice-cream* **Giorno** *day*
H	Acca (*ah-kah*)	[-] no sound	**Hotel** **Ho** *I have*
I	I (*ee*)	[i *long e sound*]	**Italia** *Italy*
L	Elle (*eh-lleh*)	[l]	**Lago** *lake*

M	Emme (*eh-mmeh*)	[m]	**Mamma** *mom*
N	Enne (*eh-nneh*)	[n]	**Naso** *nose*
O	O (*oh*)	[ɒ]	**Oggetto** *object*
P	Pi (*pe*)	[p]	**Prima** *before*
Q	Qu (*koo*)	/k/ [ku]	**Quando** *when*
R	Erre (*eh-rreh*)	[r]	**Rana** *frog*
S	Esse (*eh-sseh*)	[s]	**Sole** *sun*
T	Ti (*te*)	[t]	**Triste** *sad*
U	U (*oo*)	[u]	**Uscita** *exit*
V	Vi (*ve*) Vu (*voo*)	[v]	**Vino** *wine*
Z	Zeta (*seh-tah*)	/dz/	**Zucchero** *sugar*

You may have noticed that some letters are missing in the Italian alphabet. Officially, J, K, W, Y, X are not part of it. Italians use these five letters to write and pronounce foreign words.

Letter	Name	Pronunciation	As in...
J	i lunga	/dʒ/	Jeans
K	kappa	/k/	Kiwi
W	doppia vu	/w/	Wafer
X	ics	/ks/	Xilofono
Y	ipsilon	/i/	Yogurt, Yacht

SUONI SPECIALI
SPECIAL SOUNDS

One phonetic trait that is worth keeping in mind is the sound made by **double consonants** (*doppie consonanti*), since the same word, if pronounced with the single consonant instead of the double consonant (and vice versa), acquires a totally different meaning. Double consonants are pronounced with a longer sound.

Double Consonant	Word with one consonant	Word with two consonants
PP	**Copia** *copy*	**Coppia** *couple*
RR	**Caro** *expensive*	**Carro** *cart*
SS	**Casa** *house*	**Cassa** *cash register*
TT	**Sete** *thirst*	**Sette** *seven*
MM	**Camino** *chimney*	**Cammino** *way*
NN	**Nono** *ninth*	**Nonno** *grandfather*

Other particular sounds occur in **groups of two or three letters**. Below you will find these sounds, along with some examples. We suggest you start watching movies with subtitles in order to recognize some of these sounds and practice them.

Group of sounds	Pronunciation	As in...
SCI	/ʃ/ [shi]	**Uscita** *exit*
SCE	/ʃ/ [she]	**Scelta** *choice*
GN	/ɲ/ [gn] (similar to ñ sound in Spanish)	**Lasagna** *lasagne*
GLI	/ʎ/ [ll before i]	**Maniglia** *handle*

NUMERI
NUMBERS

Numbers	Spelling
0	Zero
1	Uno
2	Due
3	Tre
4	Quattro
5	Cinque
6	Sei
7	Sette
8	Otto
9	Nove
10	Dieci

Now that you have mastered the Italian alphabet, let's talk about numbers! *I numeri* (singular, *il numero*) from 1 to 10 are not that complicated, are they? Just practice the pronunciation, keeping in mind what you have learned about the alphabet. Let's now consider the "irregular" numbers 11 to 19.

Numbers	Spelling
11	Undici
12	Dodici
13	Tredici
14	Quattordici
15	Quindici
16	Sedici
17	Diciassette
18	Diciotto
19	Diciannove

Next stop is the tens; some are easier, some may be more difficult to remember. Just take your time memorizing them and practice with the exercises at the end of this section.

Numbers	Spelling
10	Dieci
20	Venti
30	Trenta
40	Quaranta
50	Cinquanta
60	Sessanta
70	Settanta
80	Ottanta
90	Novanta
100	Cento

As for the numbers "in between", they follow a simple logic rule. You just need to combine the tens with the numbers from 1-9 you have just learned, as you do in English.

25 (twenty-five): *venticinque*, as it is venti+cinque (20+5)

67 (sixty-seven): *sessantasette*, as it is sessanta+sette (60+7)

There are only two special features:

1. All compound numbers ending in -tré must be written with the accent.

Here is a example:

43 (forty-three): *quarantatré*, as it is quaranta+tre (40+3)

2. All compound numbers ending in –uno and –otto lose the final vowel.

Here are some examples:

31 (thirty-one): *trentuno* (instead of *trentauno*), trenta+uno (30+1)

58 (fifty-eight): *cinquantotto* (instead of *cinquantaotto*), cinquanta+otto (50+8)

Just keep in mind they are one word when you spell them (*ottantanove*, *trentadue* and so on), so there is no dash between tens and ones.

The numbers in the hundreds follow a similar rule. Some examples:

150: *centocinquanta*, as it is "cento" (100) + "cinquanta" (50).

127: *centoventisette*, as it is "cento" (100) + "venti" (20) + "sette" (7)

ESERCIZI
EXERCISES I

1) Quale lettera? *Which letter?*

🔊 Listen to the sounds and write the correct spelling of the letter.
Find the audio on page 5.

Acca → *H*

Zeta → *Z*

Emme → *M*

Ti → *T*

Di → *D*

Effe → *F*

Esse → *S*

Kappa → *k*

Bi → *B*

Doppia vu → *W*

I lunga → *~~X~~ J*

Ics → *x*

Ci → *C*

A → *A*

Vi → *V*

Erre → *R*

Enne → *N*

Ipsilon → *Y*

2) Numeri e suoni. *Numbers and sounds.*

Write the spelling of the following numbers. When you are done, practice their pronunciation using the alphabet table above. Pay particular attention to the special sounds. **Example:** 46 = *quarantasei*

4 = Quattro	59 = Cinquantanove	165 = Centosessantacinque	9 = Nove
62 = Sessantadue	15 = Quindici	2 = due	116 = Centosedici
123 = Centoveintitre	90 = Novanta	37 = trentasette	99 = NoventaNove
7 = Sette	41 = Quarantono	77 = Setantasette	172 = Centosetenradue
12 = Dodici	55 = Cinquantacinque	137 = Centotrentasette	17 = Diciasette
102 = Centodue	24 = Ventiquattro	11 = Undici	66 = Sessantasei
8 = otto	149 = Centoquarantanove	95 = noventacinque	34 = trentaquatro

IL GENERE DEL NOME: MASCHILE E FEMMINILE
NOUN GENDERS: MASCULINE AND FEMININE

In the Italian language, there are two genders for nouns: *maschile* (masculine) and *femminile* (feminine). There are few rules that apply to the gender of nouns and many exceptions! Let's try to sum up the main rules while adding new words to your vocabulary.

And how do you know if a word is masculine or feminine?

Well, either you learn that word by heart with the corresponding article—more about the articles later—or you can learn a few useful tricks.

Masculine words:

Most nouns ending in -o are masculine, as well as their plurals ending with -i: *forno* (oven) – *forni* (ovens), *zaino* (backpack) – *zaini* (backpacks), *libro* (book) – *libri* (books).

Names of trees: *pero* (pear tree), *abete* (fir), *melo* (apple tree), *noce* (walnut tree), *pino* (pine tree)…

Months of the year: *gennaio* (January), *febbraio* (February), *marzo* (March), *aprile* (April), *maggio* (May), *giugno* (June), *luglio* (July), *agosto* (August), *settembre* (September), *ottobre* (October), *novembre* (November), *dicembre* (December).

Days of the week except for *domenica* (Sunday): *lunedì* (Monday), *martedì* (Tuesday), *mercoledì* (Wednesday), *giovedì* (Thursday), *venerdì* (Friday), *sabato* (Saturday). Also, the days of the week, and months, are not capitalized in Italian.

Names of mountains and lakes: *Cervino, Monviso, Maggiore, Lario, Trasimeno…*

Most of the English words used in Italian as well: *computer, tablet, basket, film…*

Feminine words:

Most nouns ending in -a as well as their plurals ending with –e: *casa* (home) – *case* (homes), *sedia* (chair) – *sedie* (chairs), *penna* (pen) – *penne* (pens).

Most nouns ending in -i: *tesi* (thesis) – *crisi* (crisis) – *diagnosi* (diagnosis).

Most nouns ending in -zione: *stazione* (station), *soluzione* (station), *conversazione* (conversation).

Nouns ending in -tà / -tù: *novità* (news) – *bontà* (goodness) – *virtù* (virtue).

Names of fruits: *banana, pera* (pear), *albicocca* (apricot), *ciliegia* (cherry), *pesca* (peach), *mela* (apple)…

Sunday: *domenica.*

Names of the islands: *Sardegna, Sicilia, isola d'Elba…*

What about **nouns ending in –e**? They can be both masculine, such as *fiume* (river), *dente* (tooth), *ponte* (bridge) and feminine, such as *mente* (mind), *sete* (thirst), *notte* (night).

Genere comune
Common gender

In Italian, **many names are the same for both the masculine and the feminine gender** (this is called *genere comune*). In order to know which genders these names refer to, you have to look at the article (*articolo*) in front of them. We will talk about articles in the next section. Some examples include:

Singer: **il** *cantante* (masculine) - **la** *cantante* (feminine);

Relative: **il** *parente* (masculine) - **la** *parente* (feminine):

Pharmacist: **il** *farmacista* (masculine) - **la** *farmacista* (feminine);

Colleague: **il** *collega* (masculine) - **la** *collega* (feminine).

Nomi mobili
Mobile nouns

Nouns that **change their ending when switching from the masculine to the feminine form** are called *nomi mobili* (mobile nouns). Once again, there is not a set rule for this category but it is helpful to keep this in mind:

- Mobile masculine names ending in **-o** usually end with **-a** when switched to feminine.

  Some examples include: *figli-o* (son, masculine) *figli-a* (daughter, feminine); *bambin-o* (child, masculine) *bambin-a* (child, feminine).

- Mobile masculine names ending in **-e**, usually have their feminine form ending with **-a** or **–essa.**

  Cont-e (count, masculine) *cont-essa* (countess, feminine); *signore* (sir, masculine) *signora* (madam, feminine); *campion-e* (champion, masculine) *campion-essa* (champion, feminine); *leon-e* (lion, masculine) *leon-essa* (lioness, feminine).

- Mobile masculine names ending in **-a**, usually end with **-essa** in their feminine version.

  Poet-a (poet, masculine) *poet-essa* (poet, feminine); *duc-a* (duke, masculine) *duchessa* (duchess, feminine).

- Some mobile masculine names end with **-ina** in their feminine form.

  For example: *re* (king, masculine) *reg-ina* (queen, feminine); *gallo* (rooster, masculine) *gall-ina* (hen, feminine).

- Many mobile masculine names ending with **-tore**, have their feminine form ending with **-trice.**

  For example: *impera-tore* (emperor, masculine) *impera-trice* (empress, feminine); *scrit-tore* (writer, masculine) *scrit-trice* (writer, feminine); *opera-tore* (operator, masculine) *opera-trice* (operator, feminine).

Falsi cambiamenti di genere
False gender changes

Sometimes, if you change the ending of a word, you do not necessarily transform it into its feminine form. Some nouns entirely change their meaning when they take a different ending. Here are some examples:

Pann-a *cream* vs **pann-o** *rag*;
ment-o *chin* vs **ment-a** *mint*;
cer-o *candle* vs **cer-a** *wax*;
coll-o *neck* vs **coll-a** *glue*.

Nomi indipendenti
Independent nouns

These nouns have a completely **different spelling** according to the gender of the person they refer to. For these nouns, what changes is not only the ending, but the whole structure. Some examples include:

Fratello *brother, masculine* **sorella** *sister, feminine;*
padre *father, masculine* **madre** *mother, feminine;*
marito *husband, masculine* **moglie** *wife, feminine;*
genero *son-in-law, masculine* **nuora** *daughter-in-law, feminine.*

ESERCIZI
EXERCISES II

1) Femminile o Maschile? *Feminine –F or Masculine –M?*

Determine the gender of the words below.

Example: Banana = F

Divano *couch* =

Sedia *chair* =

La pilota *pilot* =

Pino *pine tree* =

Gelato *ice cream* =

Il cantante *singer* =

Bicicletta *bike* =

Musica *music* =

Pappagallo *parrot* =

Scrittrice *writer* =

Libro *book* =

Professore *professor* =

Lampada *lamp* =

Cane *dog* =

Lago di Como *Lake Como* =

Cammello *camel* =

Palla *ball* =

Bicchiere *glass* =

Madre *mother* =

Collo *neck* =

2) Aggiungi la parola. *Write the feminine nouns in UPPER CASE and the masculine nouns in lower case in the right spaces. Use the dictionary for help.*

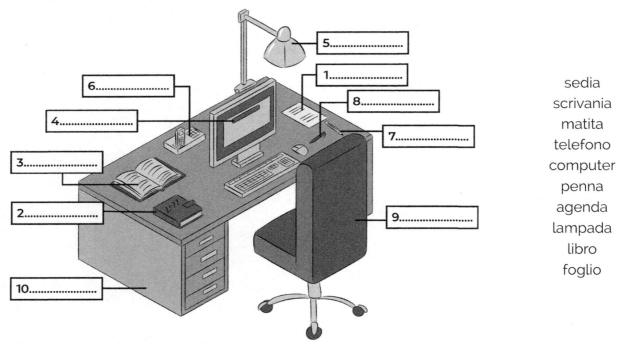

5.........................

1.........................

6.........................

8.........................

4.........................

7.........................

3.........................

2.........................

9.........................

10.........................

sedia
scrivania
matita
telefono
computer
penna
agenda
lampada
libro
foglio

SINGOLARE E PLURALE
SINGULAR AND PLURAL

Now that we have discussed gender, it is time to consider quantity. When talking about one person, one thing, or one animal we use the singular *(singolare)* form, and when we talk about more than one thing/person, we use the plural form *(plurale)*.

How do you learn the plural form of Italian words? First of all, it takes practice; as with gender, there are very few rules set in stone and a lot of exceptions. However, in order to help you find your way between singular and plural forms, you can study the list of **general rules** below.

- To make the plural form of singular masculine nouns ending with **-o**, you usually need to change the final vowel into **-i**.

  Examples: *albero* (tree) = *alberi* (trees); *cartello* (sign) = *cartelli* (signs); *piede* (foot) = *piedi* (feet); *ombrello* (umbrella) = *ombrelli* (umbrellas).

- To make the plural form of singular feminine nouns ending with **–a**, you usually need to change the final vowel into **-e**.

  Examples: *carta* (paper) = *carte* (papers); *pagina* (page) = *pagine* (pages).

- To make the plural of feminine nouns ending with **–e**, you change the final vowel into **-i**.

  Examples: *canzone* (song) = *canzoni* (songs); *stagione* (season) = *stagioni* (seasons).

- Nouns ending with **-fugo** always get the ending **-ghi** for the plural.

  Examples: *profugo* (refugee) = *profughi* (refugees); *insettifugo* (insect repellent) = *insettifughi* (insect repellents).

- Nouns ending in **-logo** that **refer to people** take the ending **-logi** for the plural.

  Examples: *psicologo* (psychologist) = *psicologi* (psychologists) or *biologo* (biologist) = *biologi* (biologists).

- Those words ending with **–logo** that **refer to things** change their ending to **-loghi** for the plural.

  Examples: *catalogo* (catalog) = *cataloghi* (catalogs); *dialogo* (dialog) = *dialoghi* (dialogs).

Eccezioni per la formazione del plurale
Exceptions for forming the plural

- **Feminine nouns** ending in **-ca** and in **-ga** change their ending to **-che** or **-ghe** for the plural, respectively.

  Examples: *banca* (bank) = *banche* (banks); *amica* (friend, feminine) = *amiche*; *formica* (ant) = *formiche* (ants); *toga* (toga) = *toghe* (togas); *alga* (seaweed) = *alghe* (seaweeds); *sega* (saw) = *seghe* (saws).

- **Masculine nouns** ending in **-ca** or **-ga** change their ending to **-chi** or **-ghi** for the plural, respectively.

  Examples: *monarca* (monarch) = *monarchi* (monarchs); *collega* (colleague) = *colleghi* (colleagues).

- **Masculine nouns** ending in **-co** or **-go** change their ending to **-chi** or **-ghi** for the plural, respectively.

  Examples: *falco* (hawk) = *falchi* (hawks); *gioco* (game) = *giochi* (games); *logo* (logo) = *loghi* (logs); *albergo* (hotel) = *alberghi* (hotels).

  However, **in words with more than two syllables, if the accent is on the first syllable**, the plural will take the ending -**ci** or **–gi**.

  Examples: *medico* (doctor) = *medici* (doctors); *asparago* (asparagus) = *asparagi* (asparagus, plural).

- For those nouns ending in **-cia** and **-gia**, you have to pay attention to where the accent is. If the accent falls on the -i, then the plural takes the ending **-cie** or **-gie**.

  That is the case of *farmacia* (pharmacy) = *farmacie* (pharmacies) and *allergia* (allergy) = *allergie* (allergies).

  Words that do not have an accent on the **-i** still have a plural form with the ending **-cie** or **-gie** if they are preceded by a vowel, like in *ciliegia* (cherry) = *ciliegie* (cherries) or *camicia* (shirt) = *camicie* (shirts).

  However, if the ending is preceded by a consonant, the plural form will end with **-ce** or **-ge**.

  That is the case of *freccia* (arrow) = *frecce* (arrows); *frangia* (bangs) = *frange* (bangs, plural).

  Some **masculine words ending with -o** will become feminine nouns in their plural form by getting the ending **–a**. This change is also highlighted by the use of the feminine article in the plural form of these nouns. Among these words, *il miglio* (mile) = *le miglia* (miles); *il paio* (pair) = *le paia* (pairs); *l'uovo* (egg) = *le uova* (eggs).

ESERCIZI
EXERCISES III

1) Trova il plurale. *Find the plural.*

Write the plural form of the following words.

Examples: **casa** *house* = case

Albergo *hotel* =

Asparago *asparagus* =

Zaino *backpack* =

Ciliegia *cherry* =

Pera *pear* =

Barca *boat* =

Fotografia *picture* =

Uovo *egg* =

Cartello *sign* =

Faro *lighthouse* =

Cardiologo *cardiologist* =

Strega *witch* =

Insalata *salad* =

Libro *book* =

2) Genere e Numero. *Gender and Number.*

Place the words in the correct column.

Leone *(lion/s)* - specchio *(mirror/s)* - ~~televisioni *(TV/s)*~~ - finestra *(window/s)* - spazzole *(brush/es)* - guida *(guide/s)* - letti *(bed/s)* - falco *(hawk/s)* - scatola *(box/es)* - galline *(hen/s)* - occhio *(eye/s)* - telefoni *(telephone/s)* - fuochi *(fire/s)* - ~~piatto *(plate/s)*~~ - cappelli *(hat/s)* - zuppe *(soup/s)*

Maschile, singolare	Maschile, plurale	Femminile, singolare	Femminile, plurale
Piatto			Televisioni

3) Trova il singolare. *Find the singular.*

Write the singular form of the following words.

Example: mucche *cows* = mucca

Lampade *lamps* =

Carte *papers* =

Coltelli *knives* =

Guanti *gloves* =

Psicologi *psychologists* =

Coperte *blankets* =

Giornali *newspapers* =

Papere *ducks* =

Tavoli *tables* =

Pentole *pots* =

Cani *dogs* =

Porte *doors* =

Pulcini *chicks* =

Navi *boats* =

Laghi *lakes* =

Mari *seas* =

Orecchini *earrings* =

Costumi *costumes* =

GLI ARTICOLI
ARTICLES

Articles are fundamental while talking or writing in Italian. And when it comes to learning them, we have some good news and some bad news.

Let's start with the bad news. While in English we only have one article, *the*, in Italian we have seven. Yes, you read that right. SEVEN. You will have to pick the right one according to the gender (masculine or feminine) and number (singular or plural) of the noun the article refers to.

What about the good news? Well, the articles follow some strict rules, meaning that once you learn those few rules, there will be no exceptions. Trust us: their use will become easier with practice, so do not get discouraged at the beginning!

First rule: articles are always in front of the noun they refer to, and they can be divided into three categories that we will explain in detail below.

Articoli Determinativi
Definite Articles

Articoli Determinativi are used before a noun indicating a **specific person, thing or fact**, and in front of nouns indicating someone or something we are familiar with. In English, they would correspond to "the". We know, it would be so much easier if we only had one article in Italian as well. And now you know why Italians love the English article, as there is no doubt when it comes to using the right one!

Some examples with *articoli determinativi*: *gli* ombrelli sono bagnati (the umbrellas are wet), *la* torta è buona (the cake is good), *il* secolo passato (the past century), sono arrivati *i* nonni (the grandparents arrived).

Articoli Determinativi *Definite Articles*	Singolare *Singular*	Plurale *Plural*
Femminile *Feminine*	La; L'	Le
Maschile *Masculine*	Il; Lo; L'	I; Gli

How can you pick the right one, then?

As you noticed in the table above, there are several options for masculine nouns, both for their singular and plural forms.

Most of the **masculine** nouns beginning with a consonant take *il* as articolo determinativo.

> **Examples:** *il parco* (the park), *il vino* (the wine), *il pittore* (the painter) etc.

We have to use **lo** for the following instances only:

- The masculine noun begins with the letter **S + a consonant**.
  Examples: *lo scorpione* (the scorpion), *lo studente* (the student), *lo stivale* (the boot)

- The masculine noun begins with **PS, PN or GN**.
  Examples: *lo gnomo* (the gnome), *lo pneumologo* (the pulmonologist), *lo psichiatra* (the psychiatrist)

- The masculine noun begins with **X, Y or Z**.
  Examples: *lo xilofono* (the xylophone), *lo yogurt* (the yogurt), *lo zoo* (the zoo)

As for the **plurals**, now they will be even easier to understand.

When you use **il** for the singular form of a masculine noun, then the articolo determinativo will be **i** for its plural form.

Examples: *il leone* (the lion) – *i leoni* (the lions), *il libro* (the book) – *i libri* (the books), *il fratello* (the brother) – *i fratelli* (the brothers)

On the other hand, when you use **lo** as articolo determinativo for a masculine singular noun, its plural form will take **gli**.

Examples: *lo zaino* (the backpack) – *gli zaini* (the backpacks), *lo psicologo* (the psychologist) – *gli psicologi* (the psychologists), *lo spazio* (the space) – *gli spazi* (the spaces).

The **feminine** *articoli determinativi* is definitely easier. For feminine singular nouns beginning with a consonant, the article you need to use is **la**.

Examples: *la casa* (the house), *la partita* (the match), *la strada* (the street) etc.

For feminine plural nouns, whether they begin with a vowel or a consonant, the corresponding *articolo determinativo* is **le**.

Examples: *le vite* (the lives), *le api* (the bees), *le ballerine* (the dancers) etc.

Now, we only have one *articolo* we have not mentioned so far, which is **l'**. You have to use it when the noun is singular and begins with a **vowel** or with the letter **h**. Whether it is a masculine or feminine noun does not matter.

Examples: *l'aereo* (the flight, masculine), *l'erba* (the grass, feminine), *l'uscita* (the exit, feminine), *l'hobby* (the hobby, masculine)

However, what happens when these nouns beginning with a vowel become **plural**?

- If they are **masculine** nouns, the articolo determinativo will be **gli**.
  Examples: *l'arco* (the arch) – *gli archi* (the arches), *l'impero* (the empire), *gli imperi* (the empires).

- As already mentioned, if they are **feminine** nouns, the articolo determinativo will be **le**.
  Examples: *l'ala* (the wing), *le ali* (the wings), *l'intenzione* (the intention) – *le intenzioni* (the intentions).

Articoli Indeterminativi
Indefinite Articles

Articoli Indeterminativi are used to refer to **general people, things or facts**, which are not necessarily known by the person speaking or to those who are listening. In English, they would correspond to *a/an*.

For example, you would say: ho visto *un* uccello (I saw a bird), *uno* sconosciuto mi ha seguito (a stranger followed me), *una* pagina del libro (a page of the book).

However, where in English the only difference is that you use *a* before nouns beginning with a consonant and *an* before nouns beginning with a vowel, in Italian the *articoli indeterminativi* follow different rules.

Let's take a look at them first, and then we will explain how to use them.

Articoli Indeterminativi *Indefinite Articles*	**Singolare** *Singular*
Femminile	Una; Un'
Maschile	Un; Uno

Of course, as in English, the articoli indeterminativi have, by nature, a singular form only. However, as you noticed from the table above, there are a couple of options for the feminine and the masculine articles.

When should you use one and not the other article? In other words, when should you use *una* and not *un'*, for example?

It is going to be an easy choice! For **feminine** nouns, if they begin with a **consonant**, then you will have to use ***una***.

Examples: una pizza *a pizza,* **una città** *a city,* **una cartolina** *a postcard,* etc.

On the other hand, if the **feminine** noun begins with a **vowel**, then you must use ***un'***.

Examples: un'ape *a bee,* **un'estate** *a summer,* **un'isola** *an island,* etc.

For the **masculine** nouns, it is a little different. You will use ***un*** as articolo indeterminativo in all those instances where you would use ***il*** as articolo determinativo and with all masculine nouns beginning with a **vowel**. Remember that ***un*** for masculine nouns is not followed by an apostrophe as is the *articolo indeterminativo* for feminine nouns.

Examples: un piatto *a dish,* **un fiore** *a flower,* **un disco** *a disk,* **un amico** *a friend,* **un operaio** *a worker.*

You must use ***uno***, instead, when you would use ***lo*** as articolo determinativo.

Examples: uno sconto *a discount,* **uno pneumatico** *a tire,* **uno scoiattolo** *a squirrel.*

Articoli Partitivi
Partitive Articles

Articoli Partitivi indicate an **unspecified quantity**. In their plural forms (*degli; dei; delle*) they are used to make up for the missing **plural form of the articolo inderteminativo** and they mean 'some'. Articoli Partitivi are formed by the union of the preposition **di** and the *articoli determinativi* we just talked about (*il, lo, la, i, gli, le*).

Articoli Partitivi *Partitive Articles*	Singolare *Singular*	Plurale *Plural*
Femminile	Della (di+la)	Delle (di+le)
Maschile	Del; Dello (di+il; di+lo)	Dei; Degli (di+i; di+gli)

For example:

- **Ho mangiato *della* pasta** *I ate some pasta*;
- **Ho spedito *delle* lettere** *I sent some letters*;
- **Aggiungi *del* prezzemolo** *He/She adds some parsley*;
- **Compra *dello* zafferano** *He/She buys some saffron*;
- **Leggi *dei* giornali** *You read some newspapers*;
- **Ho bisogno *degli* stivali** *I need some boots*.

ESERCIZI
EXERCISES IV

1) Articoli indeterminativi. *Choose the right indefinite article.*

Place the following words in the correct column.

~~Chiesa *(Church)*~~ - nave *(boat)* - gelato *(ice cream)* - zaino *(backpack)* - asse *(plank)* - gatto *(cat)* - studente *(student)* - ~~ala *(wing)*~~ - albergo *(hotel)* - istituto *(institute)* - candela *(candle)* - capello *(hair)* - automobile *(car)* - specchio *(mirror)*

Un	Una
	Chiesa
Uno	**Un'**
	Ala

2) Correggi gli errori. *Correct the mistakes.*

Find the mistakes and correct them using the right *articolo determinativo*.

For example: *Il chiesa è grande (the church is big) = LA chiesa è grande*

- **Le stivali sono belli** *The boots are nice =*
- **Il ufficio è chiuso** *The office is closed =*
- **Mangia lo pasta** *Eat the pasta =*
- **Gli bicchieri sono rotti** *The glasses are broken =*
- **I squalo è morto** *The shark is dead =*
- **I pollo è scappato** *The chicken escaped =*
- **Lo porte sono aperte** *The doors are open =*

3) Scegli l'articolo partitivo. *Pick the right partitive article.*

Example: Vorrei ...*della*...farina (*della, delle, del, dello, dei, degli*) - I would like some flour

- Devi comprare _____ pane. (*della, delle, del, dello, dei, degli*)

  You have to buy some bread.

- Ho imparato _____ canzoni. (*della, delle, del, dello, dei, degli*)

  I have learned some songs.

- Porta _____ piatti. (*della, delle, del, dello, dei, degli*)

  Bring some plates.

- Cucina _____ pasta. (*della, delle, del, dello, dei, degli*)

  He/She cooks some pasta.

- Ho perso _____ orecchini. (*della, delle, del, dello, dei, degli*)

  I lost some earrings.

- Ha bisogno _____ spazio per crescere. (*della, delle, del, dello, dei, degli*)

  It needs some space to grow.

- Ho visto _____ uccelli. (*della, delle, del, dello, dei, degli*).

  I saw some birds.

4) Dal Singolare al Plurale. *From Singular to Plural.*

Transform the following words and their articles from singular to plural.

Example: La luce = le luci *the light/lights*

- **La zuppa** *the soup* =
- **Il dolce** *the sweet* =
- **Il leone** *the lion* =
- **Il libro** *the book* =
- **La lingua** *the tongue/language* =
- **Lo stivale** *the boot* =
- **La vita** *the life* =
- **L'orso** *the bear* =
- **Lo scudo** *the shield* =
- **L'ape** *the bee* =

FALSI AMICI
FALSE FRIENDS

We all know 'false friends' are very dangerous; however, the false friends we'll talk about in this section are a different kind. They will not stab you in the back, but they can still lead you to make some mistakes. We are talking about the many words in Italian that may look like one thing but mean something else. Their spelling is very similar to that of some English words, but in most cases, they have a completely different meaning.

Below are some of the **most common misleading words**. Read them and keep them in mind in order to avoid possible mistakes!

Addiction vs Addizione

Addiction = the condition of being addicted to something

Addizione = the mathematical act of adding something

Annoyed vs Annoiato

Annoyed = feeling irritated or showing irritation

Annoiato = bored

Code vs Coda

Code = a system of symbols

Coda = tail

Cold vs Caldo

Cold = low temperature

Caldo = hot

Confront vs Confrontare

Confront = to face someone/something

Confrontare = to compare

Delusion vs Delusione

Delusion = an impression we maintain despite being contradicted by evidence

Delusione = disappointment

Fabric vs Fabbrica

Fabric = cloth or other material produced by weaving fibers

Fabbrica = factory

Factory vs Fattoria

Factory = building where goods are manufactured

Fattoria = farm

Library vs Libreria

Library = place hosting a collection of books

Libreria = bookshop/bookshelf

Magazine vs Magazzino

Magazine = a periodical publication

Magazzino = warehouse

Morbid vs Morbido

Morbid = characterized by unhealthy interest in disturbing and unpleasant subjects

Morbido = soft

Parents vs Parenti

Parents = mother and father

Parenti = relatives

Preservative vs Preservativo

Preservative = a substance used to preserve food or other materials

Preservativo = contraceptive, condom

Pretend vs Pretendere

Pretend = act so as to make it appear that something is the case when it is not

Pretendere = to expect, presume, demand

Romance vs Romanzo

Romance = love affair

Romanzo = novel

Rumor vs Rumore

Rumor = gossip

Rumore = noise, sound

Sale vs Sale

Sale *(with Engl. pronunciation)* = discount

Sale *(with Ita. pronunciation)* = salt

Stamp vs Stampa

Stamp = an impressed mark or a small adhesive used to send mail

Stampa = press, print

MODI DI DIRE
SAYINGS

Let's close our first chapter with some popular Italian sayings. Sayings often come from popular tradition, and since they are rooted in history, they offer good insight into the local way of thinking and living. Sometimes different countries have a slightly different way to phrase these pearls of wisdom; in other cases *i modi di dire* belong to a very specific culture and don't make sense for anyone else. Let's discover some of them!

Fare il passo più lungo della gamba.

It literally means to take a longer step than your leg would allow you to. The corresponding saying in English would probably be: *"To bite off more than you can chew."*

Chi si somiglia si piglia.

Literally, *"Those who are alike, stick together."* It is mainly used in a negative way. In English, there is a popular saying: *"Birds of a feather flock together"*. It seems pretty appropriate, don't you think?

Rosso di sera bel tempo si spera.

The approximate translation would be *"If the sky is red in the evening, you can hope for good weather."* We are not sure if this is a scientific way to predict the weather, but there must be some truth to it if several languages refer to the same thing. In English, we would say "Red sky at night, shepherd's delight!"

Il mattino ha l'oro in bocca.

The literal translation does not make much sense in English, but it would be *"the morning has gold in its mouth"*. In proper English, it would correspond to *"The early bird gets the worm"*.

SECTION 2

SECTION 2 - FACCIAMO AMICIZIA!
LET'S MAKE SOME FRIENDS!

Whether you are visiting a new country, working with foreign people, or just studying a new language for fun, one of the first things you should learn is how to greet people. Greetings are fundamental to meeting new people and are also a necessary first step for any kind of interaction.

In Italian, there are several ways to greet people according to the time of day, but it also depends on whom we are talking to. In this section, we will learn how to address people and start interacting with them.

SALUTI
GREETINGS

As mentioned before, greetings in Italian depend on the time of day, the relationship you have with the person you are greeting, and whether you are just meeting someone or saying goodbye.

To simplify things, we will divide the day into morning, afternoon, evening, and night. Furthermore, as a general rule, if you are talking to someone you don't know it is always better to use the formal greetings, unless the person you are talking to is a child or is much younger than you.

The tables below should help you navigate Italian greetings more easily. Obviously, the informal greetings are pretty easy as you can use *Ciao* in literally any situation, even though you can use any of the formal greetings in a more casual situation as well.

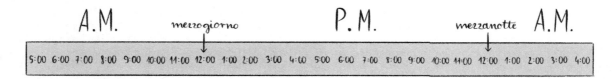

When meeting someone:

Time of day	Informal	Formal
Morning	Ciao	Buongiorno, Salve *(Good morning)*
Afternoon	Ciao	Buon pomeriggio *(Good afternoon)*
Evening	Ciao	Buonasera *(Good evening)*
Night	Ciao	Salve

When saying goodbye:

Time of the day	Informal	Formal
Morning	Ciao	Arrivederci, Salve
Afternoon	Ciao	Buon pomeriggio *(Have a nice afternoon)*, Arrivederci
Evening	Ciao	Buona serata, Buona sera *(Have a nice evening)*, Arrivederci
Night	Ciao Buonanotte	Buonanotte *(Good night)* *Used only when someone is going to bed*

The word *addio* is used in both formal and informal settings, when you are saying goodbye to someone forever or for a very long time. It is short for "I entrust you to God", *a- Dio* = to God.

Formale e Informale
Formal and Informal

We mentioned the difference between a formal way to address people we do not know and an informal way to talk to friends. This distinction is commonly used in Italy to show respect, and it is a bit hard to explain to English speakers. Not only are there different ways of greeting people according to their relationship with you, their age, or their social status, but you also need to use a different pronoun.

Generally, when talking to a friend you would use the second singular person **tu** (you). However, when speaking formally, you need to use the third singular feminine person **lei** (she/her), both for women and for men. Remember that the verb conjugation will change accordingly.

For example, if I am talking to my friend Laura, I would say: *tu vuoi una pesca?* (Would you like a peach?), or simply *vuoi una pesca?* We will see below that pronouns are often omitted in Italian. If I were talking to one of my professors, I would say: *(lei) vuole una pesca* (literally: would she like a peach?). The question would still be "Would you like a peach?", but used in a formal context. So, in these instances, the 3rd singular person is actually used for the 2nd singular person.

ESERCIZI
EXERCISES I

1) Saluti. *Greetings.*

Choose which greeting is more appropriate for each occasion and time of day. More than one answer can apply.

Example:

- **It is 3:30 p.m. and you see your friend Giulia. How would you greet her?**

a. <u>Ciao</u>

b. Buonanotte

c. Salve

d. Buonasera

- **It is late at night, and you are going to sleep. What do you say to your uncle?**

a. Buonasera

b. Salve

c. Ciao

d. Buonanotte

- **After waking up, you walk to the café for an espresso. How do you greet the barista?**

a. Buona serata

b. Salve

c. Buongiorno

d. Salute

- **You have just finished having dinner with friends and you are about to leave. How do you say goodbye to them?**

a. Ciao

b. Buongiorno

c. Salve

d. Addio

- **It is 3 p.m. and someone is knocking at your door. You open the door, and before you is an older person delivering your food. How do you greet him?**

a. Ciao

b. Buonanotte

c. Buongiorno

d. Buon pomeriggio

- **You are leaving a store, and you want to say goodbye to the shop assistant. What do you say?**

a. Ciao

b. Buonasera

c. Arrivederci

d. Buona giornata

- **You are meeting your friend Paolo for lunch, and he introduces you to his 6-year-old son. What do you say when you first meet him?**

a. Buona serata

b. Ciao

c. Salve

d. Buongiorno

- **In a few minutes, you will have an interview for a new job. The Human Resource Manager is a woman around your age. How do you greet her?**

a. Ciao

b. Buonasera

c. Buona serata

d. Salve

- **You are breaking up with your girlfriend/boyfriend. The last line of your letter reads:**

a. Salve

b. Arrivederci

c. Buona serata

d. Addio

2) Tu o Lei? *Which one would you pick?*

Underline the correct one.

Example: For the bus driver? *Tu or Lei*

- Your best friend? Tu or Lei

- A small child? Tu or Lei

- A stranger at the bus stop? Tu or Lei

- An older man? Tu or Lei

- Your grandfather? Tu or Lei

PRONOMI PERSONALI
PERSONAL PRONOUNS

Personal pronouns are very important within a sentence, as **they indicate the subjects of our sentences**, whether they are people, objects, animals or abstract entities. They are the subject carrying on the action described by the verb.

In Italian, personal pronouns are different according to the gender (*maschile, femminile*) and the number (*singolare, plurale*) they refer to. Italian personal pronouns are invariable for the first and second person, both in singular and plural, while the third person has different versions for masculine and feminine. Also, unlike in English, there is no gender-neutral Italian pronoun to refer to things ("it").

Based on what function they have in the sentence, personal pronouns are divided into subject pronouns and object pronouns.

Pronomi Personali Soggetto
Subject Personal Pronouns

Subject pronouns are used to express **who is talking, who is listening, or the subject we are talking about**. They are not used very often when writing or speaking in Italian, because the verbs endings and/or the adjectives' gender usually give away the subject. For example, if we say *Sono stanco*—I am tired—we do not have to specify *IO sono stanco*. We can omit the subject personal pronoun, and it is still clear we are referring to the first singular person thanks to the verb conjugation and the gender/number of the adjective.

Keep in mind that explicitly saying or writing the pronoun is not a mistake—it is just unnecessary most of the time. There are some instances where we do include the pronoun, especially when we want to emphasise the subject of a sentence, or when the subject is not clear (this often happens when using the subjunctive verbs, but we will discuss that later).

Pronomi Personali Complemento
Object Personal Pronouns

Where subject pronouns express the subject carrying on an action, object pronouns express the **direct or indirect object of a verb**. Object personal pronouns are divided into *forme forti o toniche* (strong forms) and *forme deboli o atoniche* (weak forms).

Le **forme forti** (me, te, lui/lei/sé/ciò, noi, voi, esse/loro/sé) highlight the function of the pronoun, which therefore assumes greater importance in the sentence.

Le *forme forti* are used for:

- All the objects proceeded by a preposition: *Parlo <u>con</u> **te*** (I talk to you); *questo libro è <u>per</u> **lui*** (this book is for him).

Pay attention to the exception! For the third singular person you need to use the reflexive pronoun *sé*, and not *lui/lei* if the pronoun refers to the subject of the sentence. For example: Pensa solo a sé (he only cares for himself), NOT *Pensa solo a lui*.

With le **forme deboli** *(mi, ti, lo/gli/ne/si, la/le/ne/si, ci, vi, li/ne/si, le/ne/si)* the pronoun is linked to the verb and its function is to make a message clear and understandable.

Le *forme deboli* are used:

- When the pronoun is not preceded by a preposition. Example: *Io **ti** ascolto* (I listen to you).

- Before the verb (and not attached to the verb) when the verb is in the indicative, subjunctive, or conditional tense. For example: *le dico, le direi* (I tell her, I would tell her).

- After the verb (or tied to the verb) if the verb is in the infinite, imperative or present participle tense. For example: *Dir**le**, dil**le*** (say something to her, to tell her).

Let's do a brief recap to simplify the Personal Pronouns with the help of a table!

		Subject Personal Pronoun	Object Personal Pronouns Forme Forti	Forme Deboli
Singular	*1st person*	Io	Me	Mi
	2nd person	Tu	Te	Ti
	3rd person	*Masculine:* **Egli, Lui, Esso** *Feminine:* **Ella, Lei, Essa**	*Masculine:* **Lui, Sé, Ciò** *Feminine:* **Lei, Sé**	*Masculine:* **Lo, Gli, Ne, Si** *Feminine:* **La, Le, Ne, Si**
Plural	*1st person*	Noi	Noi	Ci
	2nd person	Voi	Voi	Vi
	3rd person	*Masculine:* **Essi, Loro** *Feminine:* **Esse, Loro**	*Masculine:* **Essi, Loro, Sé** *Feminine:* **Esse, Loro, Sé**	*Masculine:* **Li, Ne, Si** *Feminine:* **Le, Ne, Si**

Although *forme forti* and *forme deboli* have the same grammatical function, the **choice of the type of pronoun to use** depends on the meaning you want to give to the sentence.

Look at these examples:

Forma debole – weak form

*Io **ti** amo* (I love you): this is a statement of fact. The sentence focuses on the verb; in fact I am stating that I **love** you (and not, for example, that I find you nice).

Ti vedo dalla finestra *(I see you from the window)*

Paolo **ci** accompagna in ospedale *(Paolo takes us to the hospital)*

Mia madre non **si** sente bene *(My mother is not feeling well)*

Forma forte – strong form

*Io amo **te*** (I love you): although the message is the same as before, the sentence focuses on the pronoun: I love **you** (just you and not someone else).

Vogliono **te** al telefono, non Sara *(They want you on the phone, not Sara)*

Consegna a **lui** questo libro *(Give this book to him)*

Vado alla festa con **loro** *(I go to the party with them)*

ESERCIZI
EXERCISES II

1) Pronomi Personali Soggetto. *Subject Personal Pronouns.*

🔊 Listen to the audio file, and underline the subject personal pronouns in this letter.
Find the audio on page 5.

Cara Alice,

Oggi sono andata al mare. Io non volevo andare, ma mia mamma ha insistito. Lei non è venuta, ma mia sorella era con me. Noi abbiamo preso un gelato e ci siamo divertite molto. Tu cosa hai fatto oggi?

Vorrei tanto vedere te e la tua famiglia, voi venite mai da queste parti?

Un caro saluto.

2) Pronomi Personali Oggetto. *Object Personal Pronouns.*

🔊 Listen to the audio file and underline the object personal pronouns in the letter below. Please remember that sometimes they can be attached to the verb.

For example: farLE vedere - *to show her*

Caro Gino,

Sono molto contenta di averti visto l'altro giorno. Puoi aiutarmi con il mio progetto? Ti potrebbe interessare? Fammi sapere se hai intenzione di venire a trovarmi ancora.

Conosci i figli di Vittoria? Ieri li abbiamo visti al cinema.

Un abbraccio.

ESSERE E AVERE
TO BE AND TO HAVE

	Essere *To be*	**Avere** *To have*
io *I*	Sono	Ho
tu *You*	Sei	Hai
lui/lei/Lei *He/She/formal*	È	Ha
noi *We*	Siamo	Abbiamo
voi *You*	Siete	Avete
loro *They*	Sono	Hanno

The verbs to be and to have, in Italian *essere* and *avere*, can be used alone (Sono Italiano – *I am Italian*) but they are also called *verbi ausiliari (auxiliary verbs)*, meaning they help to form the compound tenses or to switch from the passive to the active form.

Let's take a step back to explain what **active and passive form** mean.

*La **forma attiva*** (active form) is when the subject carries on the action of the verb.

For example: Io leggo il giornale *I read the newspaper*.

Here "Io" is the subject who is performing the action of reading.

Consequently, when we have a ***forma passiva***, the subject is enduring the action expressed by the verb, which is carried on by someone/something else.

For example: Il giornale è letto da me *the newspaper is read by me*.

The subject "il giornale" is still the main theme of the sentence but it doesn't act.

In order to make the passive form you always need to use ***essere***.

For example: Tu sei amato *you are loved*; **La lettera è scritta da lei** *the letter is written by her.*

For now, we'll focus on *essere* and *avere* in their present tense form. Let's practice!

ESERCIZI
EXERCISES III

1) Verbo essere. *To be.*

Complete the following sentences with the correct form of the verb *to be.*

Example: Vera ...è... in ritardo (*Vera is late*)

- Emma _____ una bambina di sette anni. *(Emma is a 7-year-old child)*

- Loro _____ felici per me. *(They are happy for me)*

- Hai visto il giornale? Noi .... in prima pagina. *(Did you see the newspaper? We are on the front page)*

- Io non _____ vecchia! *(I am not old!)*

- Il mio amico _____ in ritardo. *(My friend is late)*

- Tu _____ molto gentile. *(You are very nice)*

2) Verbo avere. *To have.*

Complete the following sentences with the correct form of the verb to have.

Example: Vincenzo ...ha....un cane (*Vincenzo has a dog*)

- Voi _____ una pizza. *(You have a pizza.)*

- Io _____ due gatti. *(I have two cats.)*

- Marta _____ 4 fratelli. *(Marta has 4 brothers.)*

- Noi _____ una macchina. *(We have a car.)*

- Loro _____ un appuntamento. *(They have an appointment.)*

- Lui _____ un bicchiere. *(He has a glass.)*

3) Verbo avere/essere. *To have/to be.*

Complete the following sentences with the right form of to be or to have.

Example: Sara ...ha... il tuo passporto. *Sara has your passport.*

- Giovanni _____ molto ricco. *(Giovanni is very rich.)*

a. è

b. ha

c. sono

- Loro _____ molti soldi. *(They have a lot of money.)*

a. ha

b. siete

c. hanno

- Il cane _____ fuori. *(The dog is outside.)*

a. sono

b. avete

c. è

- Tu _____ dei compiti? *(Do you have homework?)*

a. sei

b. hai

c. avete

- Loro _____ giovani. *(They are young.)*

a. ho

b. siete

c. sono

- Io _____ stanco. *(I am tired.)*

a. sono

b. ho

c. siete

- La bicicletta _____ rotta. *(The bicycle is broken.)*

a. hanno

b. sono

c. è

4) Essere o avere? *To be or to have?*

🔊 Listen to audio file and insert the correct version of the verb.
Find the audio on page 5.

- Aurora _____ gli occhiali.
- La pecora _____ scappata.
- Noi _____ festeggiato.
- Lui/Egli _____ allegro.
- Il panda _____ mangiato.
- Loro/Essi _____ finito.
- Marco _____ uno studente.
- Noi _____ stanchi.

TEMPO PRESENTE
PRESENT TENSE

As we all know, the present tense is used to express an action that is valid while we are talking. There are other uses of the present tense:

- To express something that happens normally as a routine. For example: *Il treno per Milano parte ogni giorno alle nove* (The train for Milan leaves every day at nine*)*; or *Parlo inglese* (I speak English)

- Something that happens frequently or a habit. For example: *Ogni estate vado in montagna* (Each summer I go to the mountains); or *La sera leggo un libro* (in the evening I read a book)

- To indicate something that is always true. For example: *I serpenti sono rettili* (Snakes are reptiles)

- To indicate activities that will take place in the near future. For example: *Domani vado a Roma* (Tomorrow I go to Rome).

The three groups of verbi regolari: -are -ere -ire (Regular verbs)

There are three main groups of verbs in Italian, classified according to their ending in the infinitive tense.

The first conjugation includes the verbs that end with -<u>are</u> in their infinitive form, and these comprise the majority of Italian verbs. The second conjugation is made up of the verbs that end with -<u>ere</u> in their infinitive form, and third one includes the verbs ending with -<u>ire</u>.

Let's see the differences in terms of conjugation.

	Verbs ending with -are Example: Cant**are**	Verbs ending with -ere Example: Ved**ere**	Verbs ending with -ire Example: Dorm**ire**
io *I*	Cant**o**	Ved**o**	Dorm**o**
tu *You*	Cant**i**	Ved**i**	Dorm**i**
lui/lei/Lei *He/She*	Cant**a**	Ved**e**	Dorm**e**
noi *We*	Cant**iamo**	Ved**iamo**	Dorm**iamo**
voi *You*	Cant**ate**	Ved**ete**	Dorm**ite**
loro *They*	Cant**ano**	Ved**ono**	Dorm**ono**

What do you need to do in order to know how to conjugate a verb? Good news, it is actually quite easy! The first step is finding the verb root, which is the part of the infinitive verb without the ending –are, -ere or –ire.

For example, the verb root of "cantare"—to sing—is "cant". Then, you have to add the current ending from the table above.

However, there are a few **exceptions**:

- Some verbs, like *studiare* (to study), and *mangiare* (to eat) have an **i** in the stem, hence you do not need to add an additional **i** for the second singular person (*tu*) and for the first plural person (*noi*).

For example, *tu mangi* (NOT *mangii*); or *Noi studiamo* (NOT *studiiamo*).

- Verbs ending in -care and -gare take an **h** for the second singular person (*tu*) and for the first plural person (*noi*).

For example, *tu dedichi* (you dedicate) NOT *dedici; or noi litighiamo* (we fight) NOT *litigiamo*.

DORMIRE | PARLARE | GUARDARE | SALUTARE
BALLARE | FOTOGRAFARE | CUCINARE | CORRERE
APRIRE | CANTARE | TELEFONARE | CHIUDERE
ABITARE | LAVORARE | VOLARE | PARTIRE

ESERCIZI
EXERCISES IV

1) Completa le frasi. *Complete the sentences by conjugating the verb in the present tense.*

Example: Viola ......canta....... una canzone (cantare) - *Viola sings a song*

- Mio cugino _____ per Roma domani. *(My cousin _____ for Rome tomorrow.)*

Verb: partire/to leave

- Io _____ al ristorante ogni sera. *(I _____ at the restaurant every night.)*

Verb: mangiare/to eat

- Paolo e Chiara _____ un libro. *(Paolo and Chiara _____ a book.)*

Verb: leggere/to read

- I cani _____ *(The dogs _____)*

Verb: abbaiare/to bark

- Noi _____ nel parco. *(We _____ in the park.)*

Verb: correre/to run

- Sara _____ una candela. *(Sara _____ a candle.)*

Verb: accendere/light up

- Tu _____ il risotto. *(You _____ the risotto.)*

Verb: cucinare/to cook

- Il gatto _____ sul divano. *(The cat _____ on the couch.)*

Verb: dormire/to sleep

- Voi _____ italiano. *(You _____ Italian.)*

Verb: studiare/to study

- Io _____ un vestito. *(I _____ a dress.)*

Verb: comprare/to buy

2) Coniuga i verbi. *Conjugate the following verbs at the present tense.*

	Guardare *To watch*	**Cadere** *To fall*	**Partire** *To leave*
Io			Parto
Tu			
Lui/Lei	Guarda		
Noi			
Voi		Cadete	
Loro			

VERBI IRREGOLARI
IRREGULAR VERBS

Some verbs are irregular, meaning that they do not follow any specific rule for their conjugation. Unfortunately, the only thing you can do is learn them by heart.

Flash cards are always a great help.

	Andare *To go*	**Venire** *To come*	**Stare** *To stay*
io	vado	vengo	sto
tu	vai	vieni	stai
lui/lei/lei	va	viene	sta
noi	andiamo	veniamo	stiamo
voi	andate	venite	state
loro	vanno	vengono	stanno

Below are some of the **most common irregular verbs**.

	Fare *To do*	**Dare** *To give*	**Dire** *To say*
io	faccio	do	dico
tu	fai	dai	dici
lui/lei/lei	fa	dà	dice
noi	facciamo	diamo	diciamo
voi	fate	date	dite
loro	fanno	danno	dicono

	Uscire *To go out*	**Tenere** *To keep*	**Scegliere** *To choose*
io	esco	tengo	scelgo
tu	esci	tieni	scegli
lui/lei/lei	esce	tiene	sceglie
noi	usciamo	teniamo	scegliamo
voi	uscite	tenete	scegliete
loro	escono	tengono	scelgono

	Salire *To go up*	**Riuscire** *To manage - to do something*	**Bere** *To drink*
io	salgo	riesco	bevo
tu	sali	riesci	bevi
lui/lei/lei	sale	riesce	beve
noi	saliamo	riusciamo	beviamo
voi	salite	riuscite	bevete
loro	salgono	riescono	bevono

	Potere *To be able to – can*	**Sapere** *To know*	**Volere** *To want*
io	posso	so	voglio
tu	puoi	sai	vuoi
lui/lei/lei	può	sa	vuole
noi	possiamo	sappiamo	vogliamo
voi	potete	sapete	volete
loro	possono	sanno	vogliono

ESERCIZI
EXERCISES V

1) Completa le frasi. *Complete the sentences by conjugating the verb in the present tense.*

Example: Viola ......beve.......una birra. *(Viola drinks a beer)*

(Bere/to drink)

- Lucia, _____ con noi questa sera? *(Lucia, do you go out with us tonight?)*
  Verb: Uscire/to go out

- Tutti i giorni io   _____ in palestra. *(I go to the gym every day.)*
  Verb: Andare/to go

- (Tu)_____che ore sono? *(Do you know what time it is?)*
  Verb: Sapere/to know

- Paolo and Andrea_____la spesa. *(Paolo and Andrea go grocery shopping.)*
  Verb: Fare/to do

- Noi _____ le scale. *(We climb the stairs.)*
  Verb: Salire/to go up

- Voi _____ aspettare. *(You can wait.)*
  Verb: Potere/to be able to

2) Scegli il verbo. *Pick the correct verb from those listed below to complete the paragraph.*

va; fa; esce (x2); dice; sa; vanno; fanno; vuole

Arianna tutte le mattine _____ colazione e poi _____ di casa e _____ all'università. Quando non ha lezione, Arianna _____ con le amiche. Loro _____ al museo o _____ una corsa. Arianna _____ che correre fa bene e la rilassa. Questa sera Arianna _____ vedere un film con sua mamma.

Translation:

Every morning Arianna has breakfast, then leaves the house and goes to the university. When she does not have classes, Arianna goes out with her friends. They go to the museum or go for a run. Arianna says that running is healthy, and it relaxes her. This evening Arianna wants to watch a movie with her mom.

CHIACCHIERARE
TO CHAT WITH SOMEONE

Now that you have learned Italian pronouns and the present tense of regular and irregular verbs, you have all you need to start **chatting with people in Italian**! Even if it sounds intimidating, remember that practice makes perfect—you have to make some mistakes and take some risks in order to learn.

Let's add more vocabulary to the greetings we studied at the beginning of this unit, and you will see that in no time you will be making small talk in Italian.

After greeting someone, we usually ask how they are doing. In an informal interaction, you will say: "*Ciao, come stai?*" (Hi, how are you doing?). In a formal situation, you will use one of the greetings (*Buongiorno, Salve, Buonasera, Buon pomeriggio*), followed by "*Come sta?*" as you will use the third singular person. Remember that when you need to be formal, the subject pronoun to use is "she", so "Lei" in Italian.

To answer this question, there are a variety of options like *bene* (I'm well), *male* (not well), *molto bene* (very good) and so on. Below are two examples of conversation in two different scenarios.

Informal:

Paola: "Ciao Maria, come stai?" *Hi Maria, how are you?*

Maria: "Ciao! Bene grazie e tu?" *Hi! I am good thank you, and you?*

Paola: "Tutto bene". *All good.*

Formal:

Paola: "Buongiorno signora, come sta?" *Good morning madam, how are you?*

Maria: "Buongiorno, abbastanza bene grazie, e lei?" *Good morning, I am quite all right, thank you, and you?*

Paola: "Anch'io sto bene." *I am good, too.*

You are now ready to have your first conversation in Italian. Note that, when answering the phone, you don't say "hello" or *ciao/buongiorno* like you would in English. In Italian you answer the phone by saying **pronto**, which means "ready", as in "I'm ready to talk".

ESERCIZI
EXERCISES VI

1) Scegli la parola giusta. *Fill in the blanks with the appropriate word.*

Mauro and Roberta are friends from college. They haven't seen each other in a long time, and they meet one afternoon while doing some shopping with their relatives.

Read the dialogue and complete it with the missing words.

- Mauro: _____ Roberta! Come _____ ? (*Arrivederci, ciao, state, sono, stai*)

- Roberta: Ciao! Sto _____ grazie, e tu? (*Male, domani, bene, stanno*)

- Mauro: Anch'io _____ bene. Questa è mia madre. (*stare, ciao, sto, grazie*)

- Roberta: Piacere signora, mi _____ Roberta. (*Sento, sono, chiamo, essere*)

- Signora: Piacere mio, Roberta.

- Roberta: Questa è mia zia, Rosa Bianchi.

- Mauro: Buon pomeriggio _____ Bianchi, come _____ ? (*Sta, signor, bene, stai, ciao, signora*)

- Signora Bianchi: Buon pomeriggio.

- Roberta: È stato un piacere incontrarvi, ma siamo in ritardo.

- Mauro: A presto Roberta, arrivederci signora!

- Signora Bianchi: Arrivederci!

Translation:

- **Mauro:** Hi Roberta! How are you?

- **Roberta:** Hello! I am good thanks, and you?

- **Mauro:** I am good as well. This is my mother.

- *Roberta: Pleasure to meet you madam, my name is Roberta.*

- *Mrs.: The pleasure is mine, Roberta.*

- *Roberta: This is my aunt, Rosa Bianchi.*

- *Mauro: Good afternoon Mrs. Bianchi, how are you?*

- *Signora Bianchi: Good afternoon.*

- *Roberta: It was great seeing you, but we are late.*

- *Mauro: See you soon Roberta, goodbye madam!*

- *Signora Bianchi: Goodbye!*

PARLAMI DI TE
TELL ME ABOUT YOURSELF

When making new friends, we often need to **talk about ourselves**: our name, our occupation, where we are from and so on. Let's take some time to learn how to describe someone, tell people about who we are, what we do, and where we come from. We will consider three separate categories: Identity; Profession; Origin.

Identity

Answers the questions *Who is...? Who am I?*

For example:

Lei è Sofia. *She is Sofia.*

Lui è il signor Brambilla. *He is Mr. Brambilla (formal).*

Sono Massimo. *I am Massimo.*

Mi chiamo Massimo. *My name is Massimo.*

Please note the use of the pronoun *mi* in front of the verb. The sentence literally means *"I call myself Massimo"*.

Also, you might have noticed that in the formal setting we used the word *signor.* When talking to or about someone we don't really know, or someone who is older or deserves a certain respect, we use **signore** (masculine) *or* **signora** (feminine). *Signore and signora* are usually followed by the person's last name, if it is known. Also, *signore* loses the final -e when placed before the name.

For example: *Signor* Mario Verdi.

The way we appear, inside and out, is part of our identity. How would **you describe yourself to others? Let's learn some new words** to allow you to describe yourself. Remember that adjectives, like nouns, change according to the gender (and often follow the same rules).

Statura *(Height):* alto / alta *(tall)*, basso / bassa *(short)*, di statura media *(average height)*.

Corporatura *(Build):* magro / magra *(thin)*, musculoso / musculosa *(muscular / brawny)*, grasso / grassa *(fat)*, robusto / robusta *(heavy)*, normale *(average)*.

Capelli *(Hair):* biondo / bionda *(blond/e)*, castano / castana *(brown-haired)*, rosso / rossa *(red-haired)*, grigio / grigia *(gray-haired)*, nero / nera *(black-haired)*. Capelli lunghi *(long hair)*, capelli corti *(short hair)*, capelli ricci *(curly hair)*, capelli lisci *(straight hair)*, calvo *(bald)*.

Barba or baffi *(Beard or mustache):* for facial hair, you can use the same adjectives that you use to describe someone's hair.

For example: La barba è bionda/rossa/castana. *(The beard is blond/red/brown).*

Colore degli occhi *(Eye color):* ho gli occhi... *(I have... eyes)* or i miei occhi sono... verdi, marroni, azzurri, blu. *(My eyes are green, brown, light blue, blue).*

Apparenza *(Appearance):* attraente *(attractive),* carino / carina *(pretty),* bello / bella *(beautiful),* stupendo / stupenda *(gorgeous),* brutto / brutta *(ugly).*

As for describing your personality or someone else's, you would normally use the **subject** (io, tu, lui/ lei, loro, noi, essi) + **to be** *(essere)* + **adjective.**

For example:

Anna è impaziente.	*Anna is impatient.*
(Io) sono creativa.	*I am creative.*
Voi siete divertenti.	*You are funny.*
(Loro) sono timidi.	*They are shy.*

Common adjectives for describing someone's personality

Noioso / Noiosa	→	*Boring*
Creativo / Creativa	→	*Creative*
Fastidioso / Fastidiosa	→	*Annoying*
Divertente	→	*Funny*
Generoso / Generosa	→	*Generous*
Impaziente	→	*Impatient*
Paziente	→	*Patient*
Arrogante	→	*Arrogant*
Timido / Timida	→	*Shy*
Estroverso / Estroversa	→	*Outgoing*
Introverso / Introversa	→	*Introvert*
Cattivo / Cattiva	→	*Mean*
Intelligente	→	*Smart*

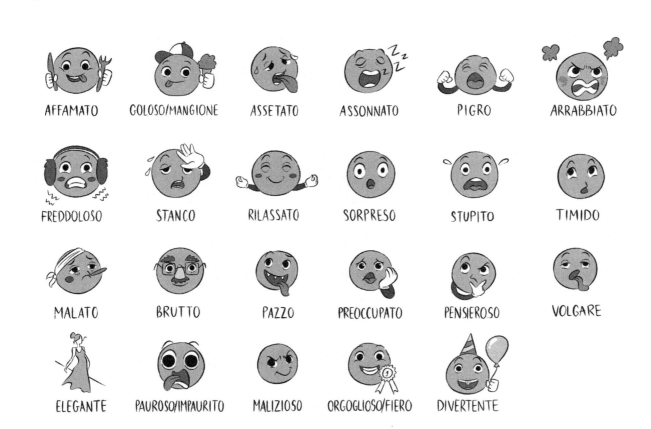

AFFAMATO · GOLOSO/MANGIONE · ASSETATO · ASSONNATO · PIGRO · ARRABBIATO

FREDDOLOSO · STANCO · RILASSATO · SORPRESO · STUPITO · TIMIDO

MALATO · BRUTTO · PAZZO · PREOCCUPATO · PENSIEROSO · VOLGARE

ELEGANTE · PAUROSO/IMPAURITO · MALIZIOSO · ORGOGLIOSO/FIERO · DIVERTENTE

ESERCIZI
EXERCISES VII

1) Accorda l'aggettivo. *Fill in the blanks by translating the adjective in the parenthesis.*

For example: Luisa è _____alta_____ (tall)

- Andrea e Alessandra sono _____ *(skinny)*

- Giulio ha i capelli _____ *(red)*

- (Noi) siamo _____ *(shy)*

- (Tu) hai gli occhi _____ *(green)*

- Maria è _____ *(creative)*

- (Io) sono _____ *(short, masculine)*

- (Voi) siete _____ *(generous)*

- I capelli di Pamela sono _____ *(blond)*

- (Io) sono molto _____ *(mean, feminine)*

2) Scegli l'aggettivo. *Find the Italian adjective that fits the description.*

For example: A tall boy = *alto*

- A shy woman = _____

- A short boy = _____

- Two creative people = _____

- A mean man = _____

- An ugly woman = _____

- A beautiful baby girl = _____

- Someone who doesn't have patience = _____

- An attractive man = _____

- A tall woman = _____

LAVORO
PROFESSIONS

One of the most common topics during a conversation is related to the **world of work**. It is, in fact, quite common to ask:

What is your job? What is his / her job? What is their job?

What do you do? What does he / she do? What do they do?

In Italy, the following questions are generally used to ask about someone's profession:

- **Che lavoro fai? Che lavoro fate?** *What work do you do?*
- **Che lavoro fa?** *What work does he/she do?*
- **Che lavoro fanno?** *What work do they do?*

Other ways to ask for the same type of information are:

- **Qual è il tuo lavoro? Qual è la tua occupazione?** *What is your job?*
- **Dove lavori?** *Where do you work?*
- **Di cosa ti occupi?** *What is your occupation / business?*

Here are some examples of how to answer these questions:

(Io) sono un insegnante. / *I'm a teacher.*

Carlo è un avvocato. / *Carlo is a lawyer.*

(Io) sono dottoressa. / *I'm a doctor. (feminine)*

(Loro) sono giornalisti. / *They are journalists. (masculine)*

(Noi) siamo scrittori. / *We are writers. (masculine)*

Maria e Anna sono pittrici. / *Maria and Anna are painters. (feminine)*

Most nouns describing a profession have a masculine and a feminine form. Like with everything else, there are many exceptions to this rule—sometimes the noun is the same for both genders, and the article helps us determine whether we are talking about a woman or a man.

For example: *il dentista* / the dentist (masculine) and *la dentista* / the dentist (feminine).

Thanks to many socio-cultural changes, the role of women is now different—women are now able to have the same professions men have. However, this wasn't the case until recently, and it has fueled a discussion on *femminili professionali* (professional feminines). Only recently, women started to have occupations that until then were performed exclusively by men, for example *ministro* (minister), *ingegnere* (engineer); *sindaco* (mayor), *muratore* (construction worker).

Languages are constantly evolving, but Italians have not come to an agreement on how to express the feminine form of certain professions. Hence, we can use both *il sindaco* or *la sindaca* when speaking of a female mayor, *il chirurgo* or *la chirurga* when talking about a female surgeon. Let's try to define some general rules.

- For their feminine form, masculine nouns of professions ending with **-aio** take the ending **-aia**.

For example: **operaio** = **operaia** *factory worker*; **libraio** = **libraia** *bookseller*

- For their feminine form, masculine nouns of profession ending with **-iere** take the ending **-iera**.

For example: **infermiere** = **infermiera** *nurse*; **cassiere** = **cassiera** *cashier*

- Nouns of professions ending with **-ista** do not change according to their gender, so we use the article to determine if they are referring to a woman or a man.

For example: **il farmacista** = **la farmacista** *pharmacist*; **lo stilista** = **la stilista** *stylist*

- Most masculine nouns for professions ending with **-tore** take the ending **-trice** for their feminine form.

For example: **attore** = **attrice** *actor/actress*; **calciatore** = **calciatrice** *soccer player*

- Most masculine nouns for professions ending with **-o** change the ending to **-a** for the feminine.

For example: **cuoco** = **cuoca** *chef*; **postino** = **postina** *mail carrier*

ESERCIZI
EXERCISES VIII

1) Unisci testo e immagine. *Connect the picture with the correct profession.*

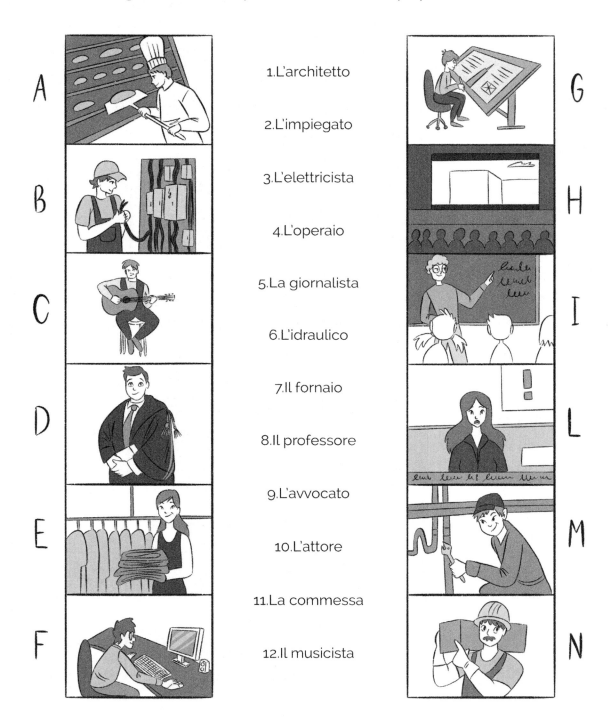

A

B

C

D

E

F

1. L'architetto

2. L'impiegato

3. L'elettricista

4. L'operaio

5. La giornalista

6. L'idraulico

7. Il fornaio

8. Il professore

9. L'avvocato

10. L'attore

11. La commessa

12. Il musicista

G

H

I

L

M

N

2) Che lavoro fanno? *What is their job?*

Complete the table with the feminine or masculine form of the occupation. Please note that in some cases the form does not change.

Giovanni è...	Monica è...
Camerier**e**	
	Maestr**a**
Impiegat**o**	
	Giornalist**a**
	Direttric**e**
Architett**o**	
	Pilot**a**
Dentist**a**	
Ingegner**e**	
Dottor**e**	
	Farmacist**a**

3) Dove lavorano? *Where do they work?*

Write the right profession next to the corresponding workplace. More than one job can be written next to the same workplace.

Cameriere - insegnante - operaio - impiegato - commesso - cuoco - segretario - dottore - ingegnere - infermiere - avvocato - manager - attrice - architetto - regista - informatico

Ristorante _____   Negozio _____

Scuola _____   Ospedale _____

Fabbrica _____   Studio _____

Ufficio _____   Teatro _____

PREPOSIZIONI
PREPOSITIONS

The word *preposizione* comes from the Latin "*praeponere*", which means "to put in front of". Prepositions are invariable; hence, their form does not change according to the gender or number of the word they precede. Italian prepositions are divided into two main categories: *Preposizioni Semplici* and *Preposizioni Articolate*.

Preposizioni Semplici

Preposition	What do they refer to?
Di	**Possession:** Il libro **di** Marco *(Literally, the book of Marco)*
	Material/subject: Il libro **di** Inglese *(Literally, the book of English)*
	How: Vado **di** fretta *(I'm in a rush)*
	Origin: Sono **di** Milano *(I am from Milan)*

A	**Location:** Sono **a** Roma *(I'm in Rome)*
	Destinations: Vado **a** Milano *(I go to Milan)*
	Target of the action: Dai le chiavi **a** Luisa *(Give Luisa the keys)*
	When: **A** gennaio vado via *(I leave in January)*

Da	**Provenance:** Vengo **d**a Napoli (I come from Naples**)**
	Who someone/something is going to see: Vado **da** Maria *(I go to Maria's)*
	Duration: Vivo qui **da** 5 anni *(I have been living here for 5 years)*
	Who performs the action: Firmato **da** Piero *(Signed by Piero)*
	Purpose: Il cavallo **da** corsa *(The racehorse)*

In	**Location:** Sono **in** farmacia *(I am at the pharmacy)*
	Destinations (regions, continents and nations): Vado **in** America *(I go to America)*
	How: Mangio **in** fretta *(I eat fast)*
	Means of transport: Vado **in** aereo *(I go by plane)*
	When: *with seasons and time of the day* - **In** primavera *(In spring)*

Con	**With whom:** Mangio **con** Vera *(I eat with Vera)*
	Tools/means: Scrivo **con** la penna *(I write with the pen)*
	How: Bevo acqua **con** ghiaccio *(I drink water with ice)*

Su	**Location:** Sono **su** Marte *(I am on Mars)*
	Topic: Scrivo un libro **su** JFK *(I write a book on JFK)*
	Destination: Vado **su** Internet *(I go on the Internet)*

Per	**Duration:** Vado in vacanza **per** un mese *(I go on holiday for a month)*
	Cause: Piango **per** il dolore *(I cry because of the pain)*
	Purpose: Uso la penna **per** firmare *(I use the pen to sign)*

Tra / Fra	**Location: Tra** la chiesa e il bar *(Between the church and the café)*
	Alternative: Scegli **tra** me e lui *(Choose between me and him)*
	Relation: L'amicizia **tra** te e Paola *(The friendship between Paola and you)*
	When: Fra un anno *(In a year)*

Preposizioni Articolate

When the prepositions **di**, **a**, **da**, **in**, and **su** meet with the *articoli determinativi* (**il**, **lo**, **la**, **i**, **gli**, **le**), they become **preposizioni articolate**.

Here is an example of a sentence in English where we have both a preposition and an article: *I go **to the** seaside*—"to" is a preposition and "the" is the article. But in Italian, what happens when they are right next to each other? They merge!

Let's see how it works:

+	di	a	da	in	su
il	del	al	dal	nel	sul
lo	dello	allo	dallo	nello	sullo
la	della	alla	dalla	nella	sulla
* l'	dell'	all'	dall'	nell'	sull'
i	dei	ai	dai	nei	sui
gli	degli	agli	dagli	negli	sugli
le	delle	alle	dalle	nelle	sulle

***L'** is used before words starting with a **vowel**, for example: dell'albero *(of the tree)*.

For example:

Vado **a** scuola = Vado **alla** scuola Manzoni (I go to school / I go to the Manzoni school)

To become familiar with these prepositions, look at the examples below:

*Gianni goes **to the** barber*	➔	Gianni va **dal** barbiere (da + il = dal)
*The cat is **on the** chair*	➔	Il gatto è **sulla** sedia (su + la = sulla)
*Give the book **to my** friends*	➔	Dai il libro **ai** miei amici (a + i = ai)

ESERCIZI
EXERCISES IX

1) Completa le frasi. *Complete the following sentences with the correct prepositions.*

Example: Ogni martedì Enzo va _____al _____ristorante

(Every Tuesday, Enzo goes to the restaurant.)

a. a

b. al

c. all'

- La lezione finisce _____ 11. *(The lesson ends at 11 a.m.)*

a. dai

b. al

c. dall'

d. alle

- Vado a Milano _____ aereo. *(I go to Milan by plane.)*

a. a

b. in

c. da

d. con

- Il nonno porta i bambini _____ parco. *(The grandfather takes the children to the park.)*

a. a

b. al

c. dal

d. nella

- Sono _____ macchina, arrivo _____ 5 minuti. *(I'm in the car, I will be there in 5 minutes.)*
a. con; tra
b. su; tra
c. in; tra
d. per: fra

- Il film è _____ cinema. *(The movie is at the cinema.)*
a. dal
b. al
c. per
d. in

2) 🔊 **Ascolta l'audio.** *Listen to the audio file and fill in the blanks with the right preposition.*

- (Loro) Vanno _____ teatro domani sera. *(They will go to the theater tomorrow evening.)*
- Francesco va _____ dottore. *(Francesco goes to the doctor.)*
- Oggi voglio andare _____ letto presto. *(Today, I want to go to bed early.)*
- Pietro incontra gli amici _____ bar. *(Pietro meets friends at the café.)*
- Ogni mattina Nicoletta prende il caffè _____ me. *(Every morning, Nicoletta has coffee with me.)*
- Luciana è _____ Svizzera. *(Luciana is in Switzerland.)*
- Vieni _____ trovarmi _____ Torino? *(Are you coming to Turin to visit me?)*
- Vado _____ università. *(I go to the university.)*
- Prendo la matita _____ disegnare. *(I take a pencil to draw.)*
- Vado _____ mercato. *(I go to the market.)*

DA DOVE VIENI?
WHERE ARE YOU FROM?

When talking about yourself, you may want to tell the other person where you are from, or **what your nationality is**. The same applies when you get to know someone else; you might want to ask the other person where he/she is from and, of course, understand his/her answer.

The question you need to ask to know someone's nationality is:

"Da dove vieni?" - Where are you from?

In order to answer, you have two options: you either say your country of origin, or your nationality. There is an important difference though.

"Sono italiano/a" - *I am Italian.*

"Vengo dall'Italia" - *I come from Italy.*

As in English, if you would like to answer with your nationality, you will use the verb to be. I am Italian = Sono italiano/a. Yes, some nationalities need to match the gender and the number of the people they refer to.

For example, a woman will say "*Sono italiana*". A man will say "*Sono italiano*".

Sometimes, you might have just an option for the singular and one for the plural. Alternatively, you can have the four options (masculine singular and plural, and feminine singular and plural).

For example, we have "*Italiani*" for describing a group of men or a group of men with some women, or "*Italiane*" to refer to a group of women only.

On the other hand, if you would like to answer with your home country, you will need to use the verb to come from. When discussing some of the Italian irregular verbs, we saw the conjugation of the verb **"venire"**, to come. If you need to refresh your memory, we invite you to look again at the conjugation of this verb.

As in English, you just need to add a preposition to the verb to come. The preposition for the English "from", in this instance, is **"da"**. "*Venire da*" is to come from.

However, after the preposition, you will always find the article related to that specific country. And what do you get when a preposition meets an article? Yes, as we have already seen, you get an articled preposition! Do you remember them?

In this instance, then, the answer will be "Vengo <u>dall'</u>Italia".

In the table below, you will find the Italian translation of several countries and the related nationalities with all of their forms.

Paese *Country*	Nazionalità *Nationality*
Italia *Italy*	Italiano, Italiana, Italiani, Italiane
Inghilterra *England*	Inglese, Inglesi
Francia *France*	Francese, Francesi
Germania *Germany*	Tedesco, Tedesca, Tedeschi, Tedesche
Spagna *Spain*	Spagnolo, Spagnola, Spagnoli, Spagnole
Portogallo *Portugal*	Portoghese, Portoghesi
America/Stati Uniti *US*	Americano, Americana, Americani, Americane
Grecia *Greece*	Greco, Greca, Greci, Greche
Australia *Australia*	Australiano, Australiana, Australiani, Australiane
Messico *Mexico*	Messicano, Messicana, Messicani, Messicane
Argentina *Argentina*	Argentino, Argentina, Argentini, Argentine
Giappone *Japan*	Giapponese, Giapponesi
Cina *China*	Cinese, Cinesi

Examples:

- **Da dove vieni?** *Where do you come from?* - **Sono irlandese** *I am Irish* / - **Vengo dall'Irlanda** *I come from Ireland.*

- **Da dove vengono?** *Where do they come from?* - **Vengono dagli Stati Uniti** *They come from the United States.*

- **Qual è la vostra nazionalità?** *Which is your nationality?* - **Siamo cinesi** *We are Chinese.*

- **Di dove siete?** *Where are you from?* - **Siamo spagnoli** *We are Spanish.*

- **Ron viene dagli Stati uniti, è americano.** *Ron comes from the United States, he is American.*

ESERCIZI
EXERCISES X

1) Da dove vieni? *Write the two options to express someone's origins using the subject pronouns in brackets.*

Example: _____ **Sono italiano, vengo dall'Italia** ___ **(io)**

_____ (tu)

_____ (noi – group of women)

_____ (lui)

_____ (lei)

_____ (voi – group of men and women)

_____ (io)

COLORI
COLORS

We have already discussed how to describe someone's physical appearance and personality. However, if you want to describe a certain object, you will probably need the **vocabulary related to colors**.

Maybe you would think that there is no grammar involved when it comes to colors, but unfortunately, the Italian language likes to make things a bit more challenging—and also more rewarding!

Some colors are quite easy, just like in English. However, other colors, like adjectives, have to agree in gender and number with the nouns they refer to; yes, you need to match the gender and the number of the noun the color refers to.

Let's take the color **blue** as an example. In Italian we say that:

Il **cielo** è **blu** (cielo = masculine, singular)   ➜   *The sky is blue*

La **maglia** è **blu** (maglia = feminine, singular)   ➜   *The shirt is blue*

I **cappelli** sono **blu** (cappelli = masculine, plural) ➜   *Hats are blue*

Le **auto** sono **blu** (auto = feminine, plural)   ➜   *Cars are blue*

The colors blu *(blue)*, rosa *(pink)*, viola *(purple)* are invariable. Other colors must match the noun they refer to.

For example, you will have to use **"gialla"** when that color refers to a feminine singular noun. *Una macchina gialla*—a yellow car—for example.

Also, please note another important difference from the English language: the Italian colors <u>follow</u> the name they refer to—they do not precede it. Technically, you can say "*Una rossa casa*" —a red house—but this is the kind of rephrasing that you would typically find in poems, and not what you would use for daily conversations with other Italian speakers.

Let's take a look at these Italian colors and their multiple forms, then!

Color	Masculine Singular	Feminine Singular	Masculine Plural	Feminine Plural
black	nero	nera	neri	nere
white	bianco	bianca	bianchi	bianche
red	rosso	rossa	rossi	rosse
yellow	giallo	gialla	gialli	gialle
gray	grigio	grigia	grigi	grigie
green	verde	verde	verdi	verdi
orange	arancione	arancione	arancioni	arancioni
brown	marrone	marrone	marroni	marroni
blue	blu	blu	blu	blu
pink	rosa	rosa	rosa	rosa
purple	viola	viola	viola	viola

Some colors have four different forms, while others only two or just one. You will have to think about the noun gender and number, and *il gioco è fatto!* (The game is made!)

When talking about colors, it can be useful to know how to describe one of them even better, for example by adding "light" or "dark". In Italian, light is "*chiaro*", while dark is "*scuro*". Of course, do not forget to change the ending of chiaro/scuro according to the gender and number of the noun the color refers to. Also, *chiaro/scuro* have to follow the color, they do not precede it as in English.

Not to mention a very important color for all the Italians... **azzurro**, which is light blue! And Azzurri is the name of the Italian football team (see the color of their t-shirt)... **Forza Azzurri!**

Examples:

Il cielo blu scur̲o = *The dark blue sky*

Una camicia grigi̲a chiar̲a = *A light gray shirt*

Le magliette verd̲i scur̲e = *The dark green T-shirts*

ESERCIZI
EXERCISES XI

1) Aggiungi il colore. *Add the right form of the color according to the noun that follows.*

Example: La sedia <u>rossa</u> = *The red chair*

- La matita _____ = *The pink pencil*
- Le chiavi _____ = *The black keys*
- I pantaloni _____ = *The dark gray trousers*
- Il giubbotto _____ = *The green coat*
- Il tetto _____ = *The red roof*
- La mucca _____ = *The black and white cow*
- I fiori _____ = *The orange, yellow and blue flowers*
- Le gonne_____ = *The purple skirts*

2) Di che colore è....? *What color is....?*

Answer the following questions using the colors.

Example: Di che colore è la tua sciarpa? (*What color is your scarf?*)

....La sciarpa è gialla....

- Di che colore è il tuo zaino? (*What color is your backpack?*)

  _____

- Di che colore è il cielo oggi? (*What color is the sky today?*)

  _____

- Di che colore sono i vestiti che porti? (*What colors are the clothes you are wearing?*)

  _____

- Di che colore è la tua maglietta preferita? (*What color is your favorite T-shirt?*)

  _____

AGGETTIVI POSSESSIVI
POSSESSIVE ADJECTIVES

Are you ready to delve into a new topic?

As you already know, possessive adjectives are very important to know and use as **they express someone's possession**. For example, when you say, "It's *my* house", you use the possessive adjective "my" to underline that the house is yours. In Italian, possessive adjectives are used just like in English, and they always precede the noun they refer to.

But—I guess you knew that a "but" was coming—there are also some differences. First of all, as you will see in the table that follows, almost each possessive adjective has **4 different forms** because you need to pick the right one according to the gender and the number of the noun the possessive refers to.

For example, "*mia*" is the feminine singular form of the masculine possessive "*mio*". If you want to say "my house", the translation will be "*mia casa*" as "*casa*" is a feminine singular word.

Do not worry—it might seem very complicated right now, but, with some practice, it will get much easier, and you will use the right possessive without even thinking about it!

What about the second difference? Well, Italian possessive adjectives need an article too, which might make things a little bit more complicated—but just at the beginning of your learning process! Of course, once again, the article needs to agree with the gender and the number of the main word, i.e., the noun that the article and the possessive adjective refer to.

While in English it would be "my house", in Italian you have to think, as it were, "*The* my house". The correct translation in Italian is **"la mia casa"**. You use "la" —as the article—and "mia"—as the possessive adjective—because "casa" is a feminine singular word.

Before adding other examples, let's check our table with the different forms of all possessive adjectives (PA).

Subject Pronoun	Masculine Singular PA	Feminine Singular PA	Masculine Plural PA	Feminine Plural PA
io	mio	mia	miei	mie
tu	tuo	tua	tuoi	tue
lui/lei/Lei	suo	sua	suoi	sue
noi	nostro	nostra	nostri	nostre
voi	vostro	vostra	vostri	vostre
loro	loro	loro	loro	loro

At this point, you might have noticed a few things. First, there is no difference between his and her as the possessive changes according to the gender and number of the noun it refers to, and **not** the gender of the owner.

If we say "*La sua penna*", in English it could be translated as his or her pen. We pick *"sua"* as the possessive adjective because "penna" is a feminine singular noun. The pen owner could be a woman or a man, but it does not matter when it comes to choosing the right form of the possessive adjective. If you really want to specify who the owner is, here is how you can do it:

Her backpack = Laura's backpack   ➜   *Il suo zaino* = *Lo zaino **di Laura***

His shirt = Giulio's shirt   ➜   *La sua camicia* = *La camicia **di Giulio***

Since in Italian we do not have the saxon genitive (Laura's backpack), to indicate possession, you just need to use the preposition *"di"*—which we saw in the previous section—in front of the owner.

Surely, you also noticed that the possessive adjective for "they" —*loro*—never changes; it is always the same form. How can you tell the difference, then? In this instance, the burden is all on the article, which will reveal whether it is the masculine singular form of the possessive adjective or the feminine one, for example.

Examples:

Il loro divano – *Their couch*. We use "il" as the article because "divano" is a masculine singular noun.

La loro macchina – *Their car*. We use "la" as the article because "macchina" is a feminine singular noun.

I loro tappeti – *Their carpets*. We use "i" as the article because "tappeti" is a masculine plural noun.

Le loro sfide – *Their challenges*. We use "le" as the article because "sfide" is a feminine plural noun.

Reviewing is always a good practice! Before moving forward with other examples, please review the Italian articles in the corresponding section of our workbook.

Some examples of possessive adjectives preceded by the corresponding articles:

Il mio ufficio	➜	*My office*
La sua camera	➜	*His/her bedroom*
I tuoi piatti	➜	*Your dishes*
Le vostre partite	➜	*Your matches*
Il nostro pianoforte	➜	*Our piano*
I loro compleanni	➜	*Their birthdays*
La mia carriera	➜	*My career*

In general, there is no rule without its exception, and this applies to the possessive adjectives as well.

The corresponding article *usually* has to precede the possessive. Why are we using "usually"? Because the only nouns that do **not** need the article in front of the possessive adjective are those related to **family members**. But be careful! This rule only applies to family members in their *singular* form. When the same nouns become plural, we need the article again.

Examples:

Mio zio	➜	*My uncle*
I miei zii	➜	*My uncles*
Sua sorella	➜	*His/her sister*
Le sue sorelle	➜	*His/her sisters*

At this point, we know that you might feel overwhelmed because of all these rules and exceptions, when in English you do not have to think much about the choice of the right possessive adjective. It will get better with practice, trust us!

A suggestion for your first exercises: when in doubt, think about the main noun first. Is it a masculine or feminine noun? Singular or plural? Then, pick the possessive adjective accordingly, and finally the corresponding article.

Example: We want to say "my chair". Chair is **"sedia"**. Sedia is a feminine singular noun; hence, its possessive adjective is **"mia"**. The article for feminine singular nouns is "la". *My chair = La **mia sedia**.*

ESERCIZI
EXERCISES XII

1) Aggiungi l'aggettivo possessivo. *Add the right form of article and possessive adjective according to the noun that follows.*

Example: My university = <u>La mia</u> università

- *Their fridge* = _____ frigorifero
- *Our windows* = _____ finestre
- *His dog* = _____ cane
- *Your TV* = _____ televisione *(feminine)*
- *Her cats* = _____ gatti
- *My mood* = _____ umore *(masculine)*
- *Your door* = _____ porta
- *Our trips* = _____ viaggi
- *His job* = _____ lavoro
- *My days off* = _____ giorni liberi
- *Their suitcase* = _____ valigia

2) Con o senza l'articolo? *With or without the article?*

Add the right article when needed.

- _____ suoi figli *(his/her sons)*
- _____ mio cane *(my dog)*
- _____ nostro padre *(our dad)*
- _____ vostri vestiti *(your clothes)*
- _____ tua borsa *(your purse)*
- _____ miei cugini *(my cousins)*
- _____ suo cugino *(his/her cousin)*

3) Trova l'errore. *Find the mistake. Read the following sentences and correct the mistakes - if any.*

Example: Il sua tavolo (his/her table) = <u>Il suo</u> tavolo

- I nostri letti *(our beds)* = _____

- La vostro cucina *(your kitchen)* = _____

- I sua pazienza *(his/her patience)* = _____

- Il tuo computer *(your computer)* = _____

- La mia vicina *(my neighbor)* = _____

- Le tua vacanze *(your holidays)* = _____

- I sua emergenza *(his/her emergency)* = _____

- Le loro storie *(their stories)* = _____

- Il vostro fratello *(your brother)* = _____

PARLAMI DELLA TUA FAMIGLIA
TELL ME ABOUT YOUR FAMILY

When you are getting to know someone, at a certain stage you will probably talk about family. That is why learning the **vocabulary related to family** is crucial to make Italian friends, especially because family is very important in Italy!

If you think of a typical Italian family, maybe you will imagine a long dinner table filled with twenty people, eating from lunch until dinnertime. And that actually happens when they celebrate some holidays all together, such as Christmas. However, in everyday life, some families still get together on Sundays, but it does not always happen. The sense of family was stronger in the past, but it is still quite important in Italian society.

After this lesson, you will be able to introduce your relatives and talk about your family. Here are some simple sentences you can use in a conversation on this very common topic.

To introduce a family member:

- Lei è mia **madre**, si chiama Anna. *(This is my mother; her name is Anna.)*

- Loro sono le mie **sorelle**, Luciana e Maria. *(These are my sisters, Luciana and Maria.)*

- Ciao Mario, ti presento mio **cugino** Antonio. *(Hi Mario, let me introduce you to my cousin Antonio.)*

Good news: the Italian vocabulary related to family members is easy and not that different from the English one!

I membri della famiglia *Family members*	
Mother (mom)	**Madre (mamma)**
Father (dad)	**Padre (papà)**
Wife	**Moglie**
Husband	**Marito**
Sister	**Sorella**
Brother	**Fratello**
Siblings	**Fratelli**
Daughter	**Figlia**
Son	**Figlio**
Stepmother	**Matrigna**
Stepfather	**Patrigno**
Stepbrother/sister	**Fratellastro/sorellastra**
Grandmother	**Nonna**
Grandfather	**Nonno**
Uncle	**Zio**
Aunt	**Zia**
Cousin (male)	**Cugino**
Cousin (female)	**Cugina**
Grandson/Granddaughter, Nephew/Niece	**Nipote**

As you might have noticed, some nouns related to family members are not so different, but only change their ending according to the gender. For example, **nonno** (*grandfather*) and **nonna** (*grandmother*). Or **zio** (*uncle*) and **zia** (*aunt*). As for nephew and niece, the Italian word **nipote** applies to both. When talking to someone else, or reading, you will tell the difference from the article: <u>**il** nipote</u> (*nephew*), <u>**la** nipote</u> (*niece*).

Two important notes:

- **False friend alert!** In Italian, we have the word "**parenti**". Do not fall into this trap, as it does not mean parents. In fact, **parenti** means relatives, while *genitori* means parents.

- While writing, do not forget the accent on the last "a" of **papà**, dad. If you forget it, that noun becomes **papa**, and now it means pope!

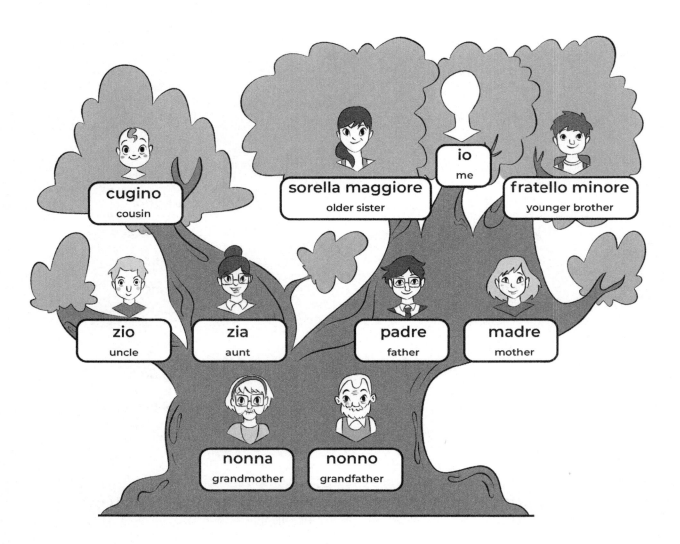

ESERCIZI
EXERCISES XIII

1) Scriviamo! *Write a short text about your family using the verb to have.*

Example: Ho una mamma, Antonella, e un papà, Franco. Ho due fratelli...

_____

_____

_____

2) 🔊 Ascolta l'audio. *Listen to the audio file and fill in the blanks with the right word.*

Ciao! Mi _____ Laura e questa è la _____ famiglia. Amo molto i miei genitori, _____ Paolo e mamma Lucia, e anche mia _____ Carla, che lavorava come _____ da giovane. Ho un fratello _____ Luca, che studia al liceo, e una _____ maggiore, Giulia, che lavora come ingegnere _____ Poi ci sono io! Studio matematica _____ e vorrei diventare una La mia _____ è tutto per me!

Translation:

Hi! My name is Laura and this is my family. I love my parents, my dad Paolo and mom Lucia, and my grandmother Carla too, who worked as a cook when she was young. I have a younger brother, Luca, who studies in high school, and an older sister, Giulia, who works as an engineer. Then there is me! I study mathematics at the university and I would like to become a teacher. My family is everything to me!

3) Con o senza l'articolo? *Add the right possessive adjective and article—when present—in front of the family members.*

Example: ... *Mia***... mamma.**

_____ genitori *(your parents)*

_____ nonna

_____ cugino

_____ parenti *(his relatives)*

_____ sorella

_____ zie *(their aunts)*

_____ fratelli *(my siblings)*

_____ nipoti *(her nieces)*

MODI DI DIRE
SAYINGS

As we did for the first chapter, let's close our second one with some popular Italian sayings. Sometimes, Italian sayings can be funny, but they offer an insight into Italian culture. As we have worked on the vocabulary related to family, you will find some common sayings about family members as well.

Would you like to talk like a real native? Let's discover other popular Italian sayings!

Cominciamo! *Let's start!*

A mali estremi, estremi rimedi.

Literally translated as "to extreme wrongs, extreme solutions", this *modo di dire* corresponds to the English saying "Desperate times call for desperate measures". We use it when there is a difficult situation for which the solution must be equally difficult.

Meglio tardi che mai.

A classic! Better late than never. As you might already know, Italians have a reputation for not being the best at being on time. This is why *meglio tardi che mai* could be the most common saying Italian people use when they are late.

Chi fa da sé, fa per tre.

Literally translated as "Whoever makes (something) on his own, makes for three". The point is that, if you want to do something well, it is better to do it on your own. In English, we would say "If you want something done right, do it yourself".

Tra moglie e marito non mettere il dito.

Speaking of family! The translation of this *modo di dire* is "Do not put your finger between husband and wife", meaning that you should not get involved in a couple's life. In English, it would be more correct to rephrase it this way: "Don't interfere between a husband and a wife".

Tale padre, tale figlio.

Like father, like son, meaning that sons will always be similar to their fathers—or more in general, to their parents. We have another figurative saying about the same concept: **"La mela non cade mai lontana dall'albero"** —the apple never falls far from the tree, where the apple symbolizes the child and the tree is the symbol of the family.

SECTION 3

SECTION 3 - IN VIAGGIO
TRAVELING

Traveling means exploring a new place, a new culture, meeting new people. It is a comprehensive experience, which might be overwhelming when you do not feel confident speaking the local language.

We are here to help! Whether you are traveling for work or for leisure, we want to make sure you have the good foundation you need to feel confident, to speak with the locals, and understand what you hear and see. This is why, in this section, we have decided to focus on the grammar and **vocabulary you need while traveling**.

DIRE L'ORA
TELL THE TIME

When it comes to traveling, is there anything more important than respecting timetables?

Imagine the following situation: you have to take a train, or a bus, or maybe you need to meet someone for work. You forgot your watch, and your cellphone runs out of battery. You *need* to know what time it is. You stop someone passing by, but this person does not speak English, meaning that you have to know how to ask the time—and understand the answer—in Italian.

You will see that **telling the time in Italian** is not that difficult. As usual, all it takes is practice! To practice more, you can try to tell the time in Italian several times a day. Simple and effective. But let's see how to do that.

First things first: in Italian, it is no use adding a.m. and p.m. to tell the time. In Italy, they use the 24-hour format, meaning that, after 12 o'clock, you will not say 1 p.m., but 13, 14, 15 o' clock etc. Please note that, instead of saying 13 o'clock, many Italians will say just 1 o'clock, as you generally understand from the context whether you are talking about 1 a.m. or 1 p.m.

However, in some cases—when making appointments, for example—it is preferred to use the 24-hour format, as it is more formal, and will avoid possible misunderstandings too. When in doubt, do not hesitate to use this format!

Now let's see how to ask the time. The question you need to ask—or that someone else will ask you—is **Che ore sono?**, which literally means "Which are the hours?". You can also ask **Che ora è?**, using the singular form of hour, but it is less common and rather dialectical.

13:00	1:00
14:00	2:00
15:00	3:00
16:00	4:00
17:00	5:00
18:00	6:00
19:00	7:00
20:00	8:00
21:00	9:00
22:00	10:00
23:00	11:00

If you are asking someone you do not know, it is always better to be polite and add a **Mi scusi**—Excuse me—before the question itself.

As in English, you can reply in two ways:

- It is 3:45

- 3:45

You can answer using the verb to be, or you can just tell the time right away. The most important thing you should never forget is that, in Italian, you need an **article** before the time. And that article could be either **l'** or **le.**

Examples:

- È l'1

- Sono le 3

You use the article *l'* only when it is 1, while all the other hours need *le.*

Le 6, le 7, le 13, le 20... (6 o'clock, 7 o'clock, 1 p.m., 8 p.m...)

Also, you will surely have noticed another important difference regarding the verb to be. When it is 1 o'clock, it is just like in English, so you use "it IS 1". For all the other hours, in Italian, we say *they are* 2, 3, 4 etc., as those numbers become plurals. Please remember that subject pronouns are not used in Italian, so you simply start your sentence with the verb.

The translation for "o'clock" is "**in punto**" — **sono le 8 in punto**, for example — but Italians do not use it very often.

Che ore sono? Sono le 4, sono le 19, sono le 13 etc.

Now, let's move forward. How would you say a quarter past, a quarter to, half past…?

- 3:15 = Sono le tre **e un quarto** *(it is a quarter past three)*
- 4:30 = Sono le quattro **e mezzo** *(it is half past four)*
- 5:45 = Sono le sei **meno un quarto** *(it is a quarter to six)*
- 18:10 = Sono le diciotto **e dieci** *(it is ten past six)*
- 19:35 = Sono le diciannove **e trentacinque** *(it is twenty-five to eight)*
- 2:50 = Sono **le due e cinquanta** or sono **le tre meno dieci** *(it is ten to three)*

However, you need to add something when you ask a question about a specific time, as in "What time is your reservation at the restaurant?"

In Italian, you need to add a preposition, and that preposition is **"a"**. And what happens when a preposition meets an article? You get an articled preposition!

A che ora parti? *(What time do you leave?)*

Alle tre.

All'una.

You answer with "**alle**" when the preposition "a" merges with the article "le", while you have "**all'**" when "a" merges with the article "l'". There are no exceptions to this rule. You always—always! —need to use the articled preposition in front of the time if you are talking about a specific event, and not what time of day it is.

Other useful vocabulary related to time:

Mezzogiorno = *midday*

Mezzanotte = *midnight*

When you use mezzogiorno/mezzanotte, you will not have an articled preposition as there isn't any article but just the preposition "a". For example, "at midday" will be "a mezzogiorno", while "at midnight" will be "a mezzanotte". As they are singular nouns, if you want to tell the time, you will say "è mezzanotte/mezzogiorno" and not "sono".

ESERCIZI
EXERCISES I

1) Che ore sono? *Write the time in Italian.*

Example: 14:15 = Sono le due/quattordici e un quarto.

- 4:30: _____

- 15:15: _____

- 17:45: _____

- 2.50: _____

- 00:00: _____

- 19:20: _____

- 6:00: _____

- 8:30: _____

- 16:10: _____

- 12:00: _____

- 13:55: _____

2) Completa il dialogo. *Complete the dialogue.*

Sara: Ciao Michele!

Michele: _____

Sara: Che ore _____?

Michele: _____ *(it is 10:30)*

Sara: Ok, grazie!

Michele: _____ *(You are welcome, bye!)*

3) Disegniamo! *Draw the hands of the clock.*

Sono le cinque e venticinque.

Sono le sedici e un quarto.

È l'una meno un quarto.

Sono le diciannove e mezzo.

Sono le otto meno venti.

I GIORNI DELLA SETTIMANA E I MESI DELL'ANNO
THE DAYS OF THE WEEK AND THE MONTHS OF THE YEAR

Now you know how to tell the time in Italian! However, if you need to take an appointment, or just have to meet a friend, you cannot forget to study the vocabulary related to the **days of the week and the months**.

Il lunedì	Il martedì	Il mercoledì	Il giovedì	Il venerdì	Il sabato	La domenica
Monday	*Tuesday*	*Wednesday*	*Thursday*	*Friday*	*Saturday*	*Sunday*

Fun fact about the Italian names of the days: did you know that they come from ancient Latin, and some of them were named after pagan Gods? For example, Martedì was the day dedicated to the God Mars, *Marte*, and Giovedì was dedicated to Juppiter, *Giove*.

An important difference from the English language is that the Italian names for days **do not require a capital letter**. Also, when you want to say "*On* Monday", you can just say "Lunedì" in Italian. A preposition is not needed.

And now let's move to the months:

Gennaio *January*	**Febbraio** *February*	**Marzo** *March*
Aprile *April*	**Maggio** *May*	**Giugno** *June*
Luglio *July*	**Agosto** *August*	**Settembre** *September*
Ottobre *October*	**Novembre** *November*	**Dicembre** *December*

You might have noticed that some Italian months look like the English ones, especially in the second half of the year—from August on.

As for the days of the week, the Italian months **do not need a capital letter** either. However, in this instance, if you want to say "*in* September" —for example—you need a preposition. The Italian preposition used for the months is **"a"** - A settembre.

Since it is different from the English format, let's now see how to write a date in Italian:

Il 7 ottobre - L'1 gennaio - Il 22 marzo

As you see, to write a date you only have to write the number of the day and the month. Nothing else is needed. Also, the article before the date will always be "il". The only exception is for numbers beginning with a vowel. In that instance, the article will be "l'" as we have already seen when discussing Italian articles.

Examples:

- *November 23rd* = Il ventitré novembre

- *October 8th* = L'otto ottobre

- *February 15th* = Il quindici febbraio

👍 Attention!

The Italian date format is different from the American one. The first element you see is the day number, followed by the month and the year.

Examples:

- *24/07/2021 = July 24th, 2021*

- *2/03/2021 = March 2nd, 2021*

ESERCIZI
EXERCISES II

1) Rispondi alle domande. *Answer the question with a date, a day of the week or a month.*

Example: Quando è il tuo compleanno? (When is your birthday?)

_____ **il 7 luglio** _____

- Quando hai iniziato a lavorare? *(When did you first start working?)*

    _____

- Quando parti per le vacanze quest'anno? *(When do you leave for the holidays this year?)*

    _____

- Che giorni fai lo sport? *(Which days do you practice sport?)*

    _____

- In che mesi vai al mare o in montagna? *(In which months do you go to the seaside or to the mountains?)*

    _____

2) Scrivi le date. *Write the following dates in Italian - article included.*

Example: August 2nd = *il 2 agosto*

- February 1st = _____
- December 8th = _____
- September 25th = _____
- May 11th = _____
- January 13th = _____
- March 6th = _____

MEZZI DI TRASPORTO
MEANS OF TRANSPORTATION

Now that you know how to tell the time in Italian, it is the right moment to introduce the vocabulary related to **means of transportation** too, as it is often associated with a timetable—*gli orari*, in Italian.

il treno

prendere il treno *(to take the train)*

la stazione *(the train station)*

il binario *(the platform)*

il bus

prendere il bus *(to take the bus)*

la stazione dei bus *(the bus station)*

la fermata del bus *(the bus stop)*

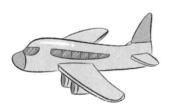

l'aereo

prendere l'aereo *(to take the plane)*

l'aeroporto *(the airport)*

prenotare un volo *(to book a flight)*

il taxi

prendere un taxi *(to take a cab)*

il tassametro *(the taximeter)*

Please note: Generally, Italian cabs are white.

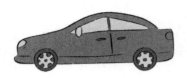

la macchina / l'auto / l'automobile

prendere la macchina *(to take the car)*

guidare *(to drive)*

l'automobilista *(the car driver)*

la bicicletta / la bici

andare in bicicletta *(to ride a bike)*

la pista ciclabile *(the bicycle lane)*

il/la ciclista *(the cyclist)*

Now you know all the **vocabulary related to different means of transportation**! However, other useful words could come in handy while traveling:

viaggiare	=	*to travel*
partire	=	*to leave*
tornare a	=	*to come back*
in ritardo	=	*late/delayed (unfortunately, very common)*
in anticipo	=	*early (unfortunately, less common)*
la valigia	=	*the baggage*
il bagaglio a mano	=	*the hand luggage*
il biglietto	=	*the ticket*
andata e ritorno	=	*round trip*
solo andata	=	*one way*
il passaporto	=	*the passport*
la carta di identità	=	*the ID*
la patente	=	*the driving license*

ESERCIZI
EXERCISES III

1) Traduzione. *Translation. Please translate the following sentences into Italian.*

- I take the train at 6 p.m.: _____

- A one-way ticket, please: _____

- His flight leaves at 4:30:_____

- I have my passport and two tickets:_____

- They ride the bike:_____

- We are late!:_____

- She leaves with the car:_____

- I come back home at 10 p.m.:_____

2) 🔊 Ascolta l'audio. *Listen to the audio file and fill in the blanks with the right word.*

Quando _____, mi piace scoprire nuove città e _____ . Vado spesso in _____ perché è il _____ più veloce e non è quasi mai _____ .Porto con me solo il _____ Prendo sempre i miei _____ online.

Translation:

When I travel, I like discovering new cities and cultures. I often travel by plane because it is the fastest means of transportation, and it is almost never late. I take only hand luggage with me. I always buy my tickets online.

FARE DOMANDE
ASK QUESTIONS

When in Italy, or when talking to an Italian native speaker, it is important to know **how to ask questions**. And for once, we have some good news: asking questions in Italian is actually easier than in English!

What do you need to do in order to transform an affirmative sentence into a question?

You just have to **add a question mark** at the end of it. That is it. There is nothing like a "do" or a "does" to add at the beginning of a question in Italian.

Examples:

- **Vai al mare domani.** *You go to the seaside tomorrow.*
- **Vai al mare domani?** *Do you go to the seaside tomorrow?*

The same thing applies to sentences with the verb to be. You do not have to invert subject and verb - you add the question mark at the end of the sentence *e il gioco è fatto!*

Examples:

- **Sono a casa.** *They are at home.*
- **Sono a casa?** *Are they at home?*

And what about answers? You have two options. The most common one is to just answer yes/no, *sì* or *no*. Alternatively, you can reply with a full answer.

Examples:

Maria è a scuola questa mattina? *(Is Maria at school this morning?)*

- **Sì.** *Yes.*
- **Sì, è a scuola.** *Yes, she is at school.*

When talking about questions, we cannot forget the **Italian equivalent to the WH questions**.

When	**Quando**	Quando parti? *When do you leave?*
Where	**Dove**	Dove vai? *Where do you go?*
Who	**Chi**	Chi è il tuo dottore? *Who is your doctor?*
Why	**Perché**	Perché piangi? *Why do you cry?*
What	**Che cosa**	Che cosa leggi? *What do you read?*
Which	**Quale**	Quale auto preferisci? *Which car do you prefer?*

As you noticed, in Italian all WH questions are quite different. However, their use is the same as in English, and you always find them at the beginning of a question. Once again, keep in mind that you do not need to add an auxiliary verb like "do" or "does" after the WH question.

Quando parti per la Francia?

When do you leave for France?

Dove comprate le vostre scarpe?

Where do you buy your shoes?

Please note that **Perché** means both *Why* and *Because*.

Perché Francesca è arrabbiata? *Why is Francesca mad?*

Perché ha perso il suo portafoglio. *Because she lost her wallet.*

Even if they do not start with WH, here are the translations of other useful question words:

how = **come**

how much = **quanto/quanta**

how many = **quanti/quante**

Which is the difference between **"quanto"** and **"quanta"**?

You use "quanto" when the subject is masculine, while "quanta" is used when the subject is a feminine noun.

Examples:

Quant**o formaggio** c'è nel frigo? *How much cheese is there in the fridge?*

Quant**a pasta** hai cucinato? *How much pasta did you cook?*

The same thing applies for **"quanti"** and **"quante"**.

"Quanti" has to be used when the subject is a masculine plural noun, while we use "quante" when referring to something that is feminine and plural.

Examples:

Quant**i amici** hai? *How many friends do you have?*

Quant**e stanze** ci sono in casa tua? *How many rooms do you have in your house?*

Are you ready for some practice with questions?

ESERCIZI
EXERCISES IV

1) Completa la domanda. *Add the right WH question.*

Example: _____ *dove* _____ **è il cinema?** *(Where is the cinema?)*

* _____ ha preso la macchina? *(Who took the car?)*

* _____ hai fatto ieri? *(What did you do yesterday?)*

* _____ va a letto presto? *(Why does he/she go to bed early?)*

* _____ cuscini ci sono sul divano? *(How many pillows are there on the couch?)*

* _____ stai? *(How are you?)*

* _____ magliette hanno comprato? *(How many T-shirts did they buy?)*

* _____ finisci di lavorare? *(When do you finish working?)*

* _____ olio d'oliva devo mettere? *(How much olive oil do I have to put?)*

2) Traduci le domande. *Translate the questions to the following answers.*

Example:

__**Quando è il tuo compleanno**___? *(When is your birthday?)*

Il 9 ottobre *(it is on October 9ᵗʰ).*

* _____ *(Which is his house?)*

È la casa grigia *(It is the gray house.)*

* _____ *(Who is their sister?)*

Elisabetta.

* _____ *(What are you writing?)*

Una e-mail ai miei colleghi. *(An email to my colleagues.)*

* _____ *(How many cars do you have?)*

Solo una! *(Only one!)*

* _____ *(Where is my luggage?)*

È in camera tua. *(It is in your bedroom.)*

* _____ *(Why does he have your bike?)*

Perché ne aveva bisogno *(Because he needed it.)*

VERBI MODALI
MODAL VERBS

In our everyday life, we probably use **modal verbs** hundreds of times. Maybe you are wondering what these verbs are, and why they are so relevant. Modal verbs are the basis for **making requests, asking permission, and expressing duties and possibilities**.

In short, the modal verbs are **volere** *(to want/wish)*, **potere** *(may/can/to be able to)* and **dovere** *(need/ must/have to)*. Before adding other information about them, let's view their conjugation as they all are irregular verbs:

Soggetto	Volere	Potere	Dovere
Io	Voglio	Posso	Devo
Tu	Vuoi	Puoi	Devi
Lui/lei	Vuole	Può	Deve
Noi	Vogliamo	Possiamo	Dobbiamo
Voi	Volete	Potete	Dovete
Loro	Vogliono	Possono	Devono

In Italian, modal verbs are always followed by the base form of another verb, without any prepositions in between.

Examples:

- **Vuole** andare in vacanza *(She wants to go on holiday.)*

- **Posso** visitare il museo *(I am able to visit the museum.)*

- **Devono** lavorare fino alle 4 *(They have to work until 4.)*

A note concerning politeness: When you are asking for something, or expressing a wish, instead of using "volere" in the present tense, it is always better to use its *conditional form*, which would correspond to the English "would like".

This is why we think that it would be more useful to anticipate the **conjugation of "volere" in the conditional tense**, as it is very important to use it in everyday life in order to sound more polite.

Subject Pronouns	Conditional of Volere
Io	**Vorrei** *I would like*
Tu	**Vorresti** *You would like*
Lui/lei	**Vorrebbe** *He/She would like*
Noi	**Vorremmo** *We would like*
Voi	**Vorreste** *You would like*
Loro	**Vorrebbero** *They would like*

As in English, then, it is always better to say "**I would like** a coffee", instead of "I want a coffee" – "**Vorrei** un caffè", instead of "Voglio un caffè".

Let's see other examples with modal verbs:

- **Posso** avere un bicchiere d'acqua? *(May I have a glass of water?)*
- **Devo** studiare per passare il mio esame. *(I have to study to pass my exam.)*
- **Vorremmo** partire ad agosto. *(We would like to leave in August.)*
- **Vuole** diventare un medico. (He/she wants to become a doctor.)

ESERCIZI
EXERCISES V

1) Coniuga il verbo. *Conjugate the modal verb.*

Example: _____ *Può* _____ **nuotare qui.** *(He can swim here.)*

·   Il mio amico _____ lavorare la domenica. *(My friend has to work on Sundays.)*

·   _____ un panino, grazie. *(I would like a sandwich, please.)*

·   Mia sorella _____ studiare il cinese. *(My sister wants to study Chinese.)*

·   _____ chiedere la tua opinione? *(May I ask for your opinion?)*

·   Franco e Antonella _____ andare all'estero. *(Franco and Antonella would like to go abroad.)*

·   _____ venire ad aiutarmi? *(Can you come to help me?)*

2) 🔊 Ascolta l'audio. *Listen to the audio file and fill in the blanks with the right word.*

Quando _____, mi piace andare al ristorante e _____ dei piatti nuovi. _____ stare attento ai prezzi, però! _____ trovare dei buoni ristoranti senza spendere troppo. _____ una prenotazione per lunedì _____ alle 8. _____ venire con me?

Translation:

When I can, I like going to the restaurant and trying some new meals. I have to pay attention to the prices, though! I would like to find good restaurants without spending too much. I have a reservation for Monday evening at 8. Do you want to come with me?

PRENOTARE UNA CAMERA
BOOKING A HOTEL ROOM

When planning to travel, you might want to **book a room in a hotel,** and you might want to do it in the local language in order to avoid possible misunderstandings.

Here we will provide you with all the necessary vocabulary to do it on your own, in Italian!

Let's assume you want to book a room, and you want to send an email to the hotel explaining what you are looking for and asking if there is any availability.

Here is a template that you can always use as a reference when you would like to book a room via email.

Buongiorno,

Mi chiamo _____ e vorrei prenotare una stanza singola/doppia per tre notti a partire dal 15 luglio. Avete disponibilità in quella data? Può fornirmi qualche informazione sui prezzi?

Vi ringrazio in anticipo,

Cordiali saluti,

_____

Translation:

Good morning,

My name is _____ and I would like to book a single/double room for three nights starting from July 15th. Do you have any rooms available for that period? Could you provide me with some info on the prices?

Thanks in advance,

Best regards,

Of course, when it comes to booking a hotel, you should know some **specific vocabulary**. Let's discover it:

la camera	=	*room*	**colazione inclusa**	=	*breakfast included*
la chiave	=	*key*	**parcheggio**	=	*parking*
camera singola	=	*single room*	**il prezzo/la tariffa**	=	*the price*
camera doppia	=	*double room*	**le date**	=	*dates*
camera tripla	=	*triple room*	**dal... al...**	=	*from... to...*
prenotare	=	*to book*	**le persone**	=	*people*
la notte	=	*night*	**l'adulto/gli adulti**	=	*adult(s)*
disponibilità	=	*availability*	**il bambino/i**	=	*child/children*
mezza pensione	=	*half board*	**fare il check in**	=	*to check in*
pensione completa	=	*full board*	**fare il check out**	=	*to check out*

ESERCIZI
EXERCISES VI

1) Scrivi un'email. *Write an email to a hotel in Rome to book a room. Mention and ask for the following information:*

- Room for 3 people, 2 adults and 1 child
- Dates: from June 14th to June 17th
- Breakfast included
- Ask if there is a parking lot
- Ask if you can check out at midday

PRENOTARE UN TAVOLO
BOOKING A TABLE

When you would like **to book a table at a local Italian restaurant**, it is quite unlikely that you are going to send an email. The easiest way is to call. We know that a phone call in a foreign language could sound quite scary, but fear not: we can assure you that an average call to book a table can be as short as just two minutes.

As we did for booking a hotel, we will show you an example of a typical **call to book a table**.

- *Cameriere:* Pronto?

- *Tu:* Buongiorno/Buonasera, vorrei prenotare un tavolo per quattro persone sabato sera, verso le otto e trenta se avete posto.

- *Cameriere:* Mi lasci controllare… Sì, abbiamo un tavolo. A che nome?

- *Tu:* Smith.

- *Cameriere:* Perfetto, a sabato allora. Arrivederci!

- *Tu:* Grazie, arrivederci.

Translation:

Waiter: Hello?

You: Good morning/good evening, I would like to book a table for four people, on Saturday evening, around 8:30, if possible.

Waiter: Let me check… Yes, we have a table. Can I get a name?

You: Smith.

Waiter: Perfect, see you on Saturday then. Goodbye!

You: Thank you, goodbye.

Ecco fatto! *– that's it! There is no reason to be nervous. Just follow these guidelines, and you will be ready to enjoy your forthcoming lunch/dinner out!*

ESERCIZI
EXERCISES VII

1) 🔊 Ascolta l'audio. *Listen to the audio file and fill in the blanks with the right words/sentences.*

- _____

- Buongiorno! _____ un tavolo per domenica a _____ Avete posto?

- Buongiorno _____ Si, abbiamo posto. Per quante _____ ?

- Siamo in _____ È possibile?

- Certamente. _____ ?

- _____

- Benissimo, a domenica!

- A domenica, _____ !

Translation:

- *Hello?*

- *Good morning! I would like a table for Sunday, at lunch. Do you have a free table?*

- *Good morning madam. Yes, we have one. For how many people?*

- *We are five. Is it possible?*

- *Of course. What time?*

- *At 1 p.m.*

- *Perfect, see you on Sunday!*

- *See you on Sunday, goodbye!*

ORDINARE AL RISTORANTE
ORDERING IN A RESTAURANT

You called to book your table in an Italian restaurant, and now it is time to go and enjoy your dinner/lunch out! Maybe you are wondering whether the waiters in the restaurant speak English, and the idea of ordering your food in Italian may sound a bit stressful.

But fear not: if you are in one of the major Italian cities, it is likely that at least one person in that restaurant will speak English!

In any case, it is always a good idea to **learn how to order your food in Italian**, not only to be sure about what you are going to get in your dish, but also because it is definitely useful vocabulary!

In this section we will give you some useful tips. Maybe you already know that, when it comes to food, Italians follow some strict unspoken rules. Keep on reading if you are eager to discover how not to make any foreigner "mistakes" when ordering your food in an Italian restaurant!

First, which are the different sections that you are going to find on an Italian menu?

The **antipasti** are the appetizers. In general, you have the *antipasti* and then a main course. It is quite uncommon to order just the *antipasti* when you are in a restaurant, even if sometimes servings are HUGE!

👉 **Useful tip:** We know, when you sit at a restaurant table, you start getting hungrier and hungrier. However, when you get your *antipasti*, do not overeat—even if it is tempting! You will not be able to enjoy the rest of the meal, as you would feel like you have eaten too much already.

Then you will order your main course. You can order a pasta dish—of course! —and/or a salad, meat, fish, or other vegetables, according to what is available on the menu.

Starting with **pasta**, you could have two separate sections on the menu:

Primi di terra = Pasta dishes of the land (mainly with meat or some vegetables)

Primi di mare = Pasta dishes of the sea

👉 **Useful tip:** Never ask for parmesan/cheese if you order pasta with seafood! Italians are serious about it.

When ordering your food, always follow the "sacred" order:

Appetizers—main course—side dish (**contorni**)

When it comes to dessert, in general a waiter will come to your table to ask if you would like to have one, once you have finished eating what you already ordered. Same for coffee.

👍 **Useful tip:** Italians would never—NEVER! —order a cappuccino at the end of a meal. Traditionally, *cappuccini* are meant for breakfast only.

It will be up to you to ask the waiter for your check—*il conto*—as bringing it directly to your table is seen as impolite. Once asked, the waiter will bring the check to your table or will ask you to come pay at the counter—*alla cassa*.

If you remember, we have already discussed the importance of being polite when asking for something. When you are at a restaurant, then, you should always use the conditional tense of to want—*vorrei* etc.

Now that we have covered the basics, let's see/review some useful vocabulary before showing you a practical example!

prenotazione	=	*booking*
ordinare	=	*to order*
antipasti	=	*appetizers*
primi piatti	=	*pasta/rice dishes*
secondi piatti	=	*main course with meat, fish or a vegetarian option*
contorni	=	*side dishes*
insalatone	=	*salads*
dolci/dessert	=	*desserts*
bibite/bevande	=	*beverages*
acqua naturale	=	*still water*
acqua frizzante	=	*sparkling water*
vino bianco/rosso	=	*white/red wine*
birra	=	*beer*
una bottiglia di...	=	*a bottle of...*
un bicchiere di...	=	*a glass of...*
conto	=	*check*
pagare	=	*to pay*
in contanti	=	*in cash*
con la carta di credito	=	*by credit card*

Bad news: in Italian restaurants, you have to pay for water!

Now, let's see two examples of a conversation between a waiter and a customer in a restaurant.

1) Cameriere: Buongiorno, ha deciso cosa ordinare?

Cliente: Sì, sono pronto!

Cameriere: Perfetto, mi dica.

Cliente: Vorrei un mix di crostini come antipasto, poi le tagliatelle al tartufo e verdure alla griglia.

Cameriere: Benissimo. Da bere?

Cliente: Un bicchiere di vino rosso e una bottiglia di acqua naturale, grazie.

Cameriere: Ottimo, grazie mille.

Translation:

Waiter: Good morning, have you decided what to order?

Customer: Yes, I'm ready!

Waiter: Perfect, I am all ears.

Customer: I would like a crostini mix as appetizer, then truffle tagliatelle and grilled vegetables.

Waiter: Great. What would you like to drink?

Customer: A glass of red wine and a bottle of still water, please.

Waiter: That's perfect, thank you very much.

2) *Cliente:* Mi scusi, posso avere il conto per favore?

Cameriera: Certamente, glielo porto subito.

.....

Cameriera: Ecco a lei.

Cliente: Grazie. Posso pagare con la carta?

Cameriera: Si, certo, ma deve andare alla cassa.

Cliente: Perfetto, la ringrazio.

Translation:

Customer: Excuse me, may I have the check please?

Waitress: *Of course, I'll bring it to you right away.*

......

Waitress: *Here you are.*

Customer: Thank you. Can I pay by credit card?

Waitress: *Yes, of course, but you have to go to the counter.*

Customer: Perfect, thank you.

ESERCIZI
EXERCISES VIII

1) Traduzione. *Translate the following sentences into Italian.*

- I would like a pizza and a beer, please.

  _____

- Can I pay in cash?

  _____

- We would like two glasses of wine, please.

  _____

- I would like a pasta dish with salmon (salmone), and she would like a salad with tuna (tonno).

  _____

2) 🔊 Ascolta l'audio. *Listen to the audio file and fill in the blanks with the right words/sentences.*

- Buongiorno! _____ per ordinare?
- Sì! _____ prosciutto e melone come _____ e due piatti di _____
- Perfetto. Cosa vi porto da _____?
- Una _____ d'acqua naturale, grazie.
- Benissimo. _____

Translation:

- Good afternoon! Are you ready to order?
- Yes! We will take ham and melon as appetizers, and two pasta dishes with clams.
- Perfect. What shall I bring you to drink?
- A bottle of still water, please.
- Great. See you later.

IL CIBO
FOOD

You probably knew that this section was coming! After discussing how to book a table and how to order in a restaurant, we should definitely look into **the vocabulary related to one of the most beautiful things Italy has to offer, *il cibo!***

Of course, we are not going to translate every single Italian food—otherwise this workbook would become a dictionary! —but we will do the main ones, so that you can really feel comfortable while ordering your delicious food.

If you are hungry, maybe it would be better to read all this vocabulary after having eaten something. This list will make your mouth water!

carne	=	*meat*
maiale	=	*pork*
manzo	=	*beef*
agnello	=	*lamb*
cinghiale	=	*boar*
pollo	=	*chicken*
tacchino	=	*turkey*
prosciutto	=	*ham*
salame	=	*salami*
salame piccante	=	*spicy salami*
salsicce	=	*sausages*
hamburger	=	*burger*
cotoletta	=	*cutlet*

pesce e frutti di mare	=	*fish and seafood*
tonno	=	*tuna*
salmone	=	*salmon*
vongole	=	*clams*
cozze	=	*mussels*
polpo	=	*octopus*
calamari	=	*squid*
spigola	=	*seabass*
pesce spada	=	*swordfish*
merluzzo	=	*cod*
verdure	=	*vegetables*
patate	=	*potatoes*
patatine fritte	=	*french fries*
patate dolci	=	*sweet potatoes*
pomodori	=	*tomatoes*
melanzane	=	*eggplants*
zucchine	=	*zucchini*
peperoni	=	*bell pepper*
cipolla	=	*onion*
insalata	=	*salad*
cavolo	=	*cabbage*
cavolfiore	=	*cauliflower*
carote	=	*carrots*
carciofi	=	*artichokes*

dolci	=	*desserts*
torta	=	*cake*
biscotti	=	cookies
gelato	=	*ice cream*
vegetariano	=	*vegetarian*
vegano	=	*vegan*

Important note: when using *vegetariano* or *vegano*, please remember to change their ending according to the gender and the number of the subject(s)!

Examples:

Sono vegan**o** – *I am vegan (masculine)*

Lei è vegan**a** – *She is vegan (feminine)*

Siamo vegan**i** – *We are vegan ("we" as group of men or a group of men with some women)*

Now you know (almost) everything about Italian food! The only thing left is to enjoy it.

Buon appetito! – *Enjoy your meal!*

ESERCIZI
EXERCISES IX

1) Aggiungi l'articolo. *Add the right article in front of the food. Tip: pay attention to the word ending!*

Example: ___ le ___ carote

- _____ maiale
- _____ polli
- _____ spigola
- _____ patate
- _____ tonno
- _____ cavoli
- _____ carciofi
- _____ insalata
- _____ peperone

2) Ti piace o non ti piace? *Add the foods that you like (mi piace) and do not like (non mi piace) in the following table.*

Mi piace	Non mi piace

I VERBI RIFLESSIVI
REFLEXIVE VERBS

Do not worry, you already know them! In short, reflexive verbs are **verbs whose subject and object are the same**. For example, "I wash myself" is a reflexive verb, whose subject and object is always "me".

In Italian, reflexive verbs are more common than in English, and they are often used to describe something you would do during the day.

In English, reflexive verbs are always followed by the corresponding reflexive pronouns (myself, yourself etc.). The same applies in Italian as well.

Let's now discover the translation of the reflexive pronouns in Italian.

Subject pronoun	Reflexive pronoun ENG	Reflexive pronoun ITA
Io *(I)*	*myself*	**mi**
Tu *(you)*	*yourself*	**ti**
Lui *(he)* / Lei *(she)*	*himself / herself*	**si**
Noi *(we)*	*ourselves*	**ci**
Voi *(you)*	*yourselves*	**vi**
Loro *(they)*	*themselves*	**si**

You might have noticed a few things. First, the Italian reflexive pronouns are much shorter than the English ones!

Then, if you take a closer look, you will notice that not only is the reflexive pronoun for "he" and "she" the same, but it is the same for "they" as well—**si**.

Please note this difference from English: Generally, in Italian, **the reflexive pronouns precede the reflexive verb**, and do not follow it. We will see some examples in a bit.

However, before showing you some examples, maybe you are asking yourself a very important question: How can you recognize reflexive verbs in Italian?

When it comes to conjugated verbs, it is quite easy, as you will immediately spot one of the reflexive pronouns shown in the table above.

And when it comes to the base form of a verb, it is even easier! As already explained, in Italian the three groups of verbs have the *-are, -ere, -ire* endings, respectively.

What about reflexive verbs, then? Do they have the same ending?

The answer is no. In their base form, reflexive verbs still belong to one of the three groups, but they always **end with the suffix –si**. Please note that some Italian reflexive verbs are not equally reflexive in English.

Examples:

Lavarsi (Lavare + -si) = *to wash yourself*

Alzarsi (Alzare + -si) = *to get up*

Vestirsi (Vestire + -si) = *to get dressed*

When you conjugate the reflexive verb, then, you will simply have to use the same endings we saw for each group of verbs. For *alzarsi*, you will take the verb root – *alz* – and you will have to add the endings of the –*are* verbs.

To make it clear, let's look at the conjugation of *lavarsi*.

Lavarsi

Io mi lavo *I wash myself*

Tu ti lavi *you wash yourself*

lui/lei/Lei si lava *he/she washes himself/herself*

Noi ci laviamo *we wash ouselves*

Voi vi lavate *you wash yourselves*

Loro si lavano *they wash temselves*

Long story short: when you conjugate a reflexive verb, the only thing you have to remember is to **add the reflexive pronoun**!

One last thing about these verbs. In Italian, a reflexive verb can also express a **reciprocal action**, or an action involving two (or more) people. In this instance, these verbs are called *verbi reciproci*.

Examples:

*   **sposarsi** = *to get married*
*   **chiamarsi** = *to call each other*
*   **conoscersi** = *to know each other*
*   **innamorarsi** = *to fall in love*
*   **incontrarsi** = *to meet*
*   **amarsi** = *to love each other*

Think about one of our first sections, when we taught you how to introduce yourself in Italian. In fact, the sentence to introduce yourself is "Mi chiamo…." Do you remember?

Now you know that chiamarsi is a reflexive verb! We could literally translate it as "I call myself…"

ESERCIZI
EXERCISES X

1) Traduzione. *Translate the following verbs into Italian.*

Example: You regret (pentirsi) = *Ti penti*

- I wash myself (lavarsi) = _____
- We meet (incontrarsi) = _____
- They fall in love (innamorarsi) = _____
- You get up (alzarsi) = _____
- She gets dressed (vestirsi) = _____
- They get married (sposarsi) = _____
- My name is Marco (chiamarsi) = _____

2) Abitudini mattutine. *What is your morning routine? Write a short text about your habits in the morning.*

_____

_____

_____

_____

_____

Example:

La mattina mi sveglio abbastanza presto, verso le 7 e mezzo. Mi faccio una doccia per iniziare la giornata con il piede giusto. Poi faccio colazione in cucina; mangio uno yogurt e bevo un succo di frutta. Mi preparo per andare al lavoro e poi esco.

Translation:

In the morning, I wake up (svegliarsi) quite early, around 7:30. I take a shower (farsi una doccia) to start the day on the right foot. Then I have breakfast in the kitchen—I eat a yogurt and I drink a juice. I get ready (prepararsi) to go to work and I leave the house.

3) Coniuga il verbo. *Write the conjugation of the reflexive verbs of the example above.*

- Svegliarsi

_____

_____

_____

_____

_____

_____

- Farsi

_____

_____

_____

_____

_____

_____

- Prepararsi

_____

_____

_____

_____

_____

_____

LA CITTÀ
THE CITY

As in the next section we are going to focus on **giving and asking for directions**—spoiler alert! —we should work on the vocabulary related to the city first.

If you are going to Italy as a tourist, or if you are moving there, it is of the utmost importance to know **what to call places** within the city in Italian. Also, if you are traveling to small cities, it is likely that all signs are going to be in Italian only, without any English translations.

You could visit *una* **città**—a city—or **un paese** – a village. Please note the accent on the last letter of **città**. We remind you that, in Italian, if there is an accent, it is always going to be on the last letter of a word, and it actually shows you how to pronounce that word.

Cosa troviamo in una città? – *What do we find in a city?*

il comune

the town hall

la scuola

the school

la banca

the bank

la posta

the post office

il cinema

the cinema

il parco

the park

il museo

the museum

la palestra

the gym

il supermercato

the supermarket

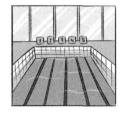

la piscina

the swimming pool

il negozio

the shop

l'ospedale

the hospital

il parcheggio

the parking lot

la spiaggia

the beach

la stazione di polizia

the police station

ESERCIZI
EXERCISES XI

1) Rispondi alle domande. *Answer the following questions.*

Example: Dove vai per comprare l'acqua? *(Where do you go to buy water?)* ____ **Supermercato** ____

- Dove vai per inviare una cartolina? *(Where do you go to send a postcard?)*

_____

- Dove vai per nuotare? *(Where do you go to swim?)*

_____

- Dove vai per guardare un film? *(Where do you go to watch a movie?)*

_____

- Dove vai per parlare con il sindaco? *(Where do you go to speak with the mayor?)*

_____

- Dove vai per vedere una mostra? *(Where do you go to see an art exhibition?)*

_____

- Dove vai per portare fuori il cane? *(Where do you go to walk the dog?)*

_____

2) 🔊 Ascolta l'audio. *Listen to the audio file and fill in the blanks with the right words.*

Abito in una piccola _____ vicino Milano. Non ci sono molti _____ ma abbiamo una _____ e un _____ abbastanza grande. Il mio posto _____ è il _____ locale, in cui è possibile ammirare molte _____ antiche. Ci sono anche tre _____ e un _____ enorme che mi piace molto.

Translation:

I live in a small city near Milan. There are not many shops, but we have a swimming pool and quite a big cinema. My favorite place is the local museum, where you can admire many ancient statues. There are three schools too and a huge park that I love.

CHIEDERE E DARE INDICAZIONI
GIVING AND ASKING FOR DIRECTIONS

When in Italy, you might need to **ask for directions**, and it is possible that the person you ask does not speak English. Why not try to ask for directions in Italian right away?

Do not worry, Italians will be happy to help you, and they will not judge you if you happen to make a few mistakes while talking in their language! They will appreciate your effort in any case.

First things first. How should you ask for directions?

The **standard question** you would ask is:

Mi scusi, dov'è/dove sono...?

- Excuse me, where is/where are...?

As you are probably asking someone that you do not know, it is always better to use the courtesy form, and refer to the other person as *Lei*—she—as we have already discussed.

If you are asking someone younger, whether it is a teenager or maybe someone in his/her early 20s, you can be less formal.

In this instance, you can say:

Scusami, dov'è/dove sono...?

In the English translation, there is no real difference between this question and the previous one. However, in Italian, it makes a huge difference as it shows your politeness.

Now, let's see the useful **vocabulary related to street directions** in Italian:

andare sempre dritto	=	*to go straight on*
strada/via	=	*street*
piazza	=	*square*
girare a	=	*to turn*
destra	=	*right*
sinistra	=	*left*
oltrepassare	=	*to go beyond*
di fronte a	=	*in front of*
dietro a	=	*behind*
accanto a	=	*next to*
tra	=	*between*
vicino	=	*near*
lontano	=	*far*
semaforo	=	*traffic light*
rotonda	=	*roundabout*

ⓘ **Note:** Please pay attention when using **di fronte a, dietro a, accanto a**. The preposition **a** will merge with the article of the following noun, thus creating an articled preposition.

Examples:

- Di fronte **a** + **la** chiesa = Di fronte **alla** chiesa *(In front of the church)*
- Dietro **a** + **il** comune = Dietro **al** comune *(Behind the town hall)*

Are you feeling ready to give and ask for directions now? Let's practice!

ESERCIZI
EXERCISES XII

1) Dov'è...? *Look at the map and answer the following questions.*

Example: Dov'è la fontana? *(Where is the fountain?)* **...La fontana è dietro il parcheggio...** *(The fountain is behind the parking lot)*

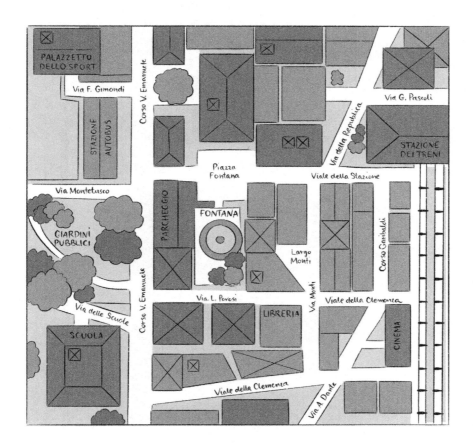

- **Dov'è il palazzetto dello sport?** *Where is the sports arena?*

_____

- **Dov'è Piazza Fontana?** *Where is Fontana Square?*

_____

- **Dov'è la stazione dei treni?** *Where is the train station?*

_____

- **Dove sono i giardini pubblici?** *Where are the public gardens?*

_____

2) Osserva la cartina. *Look at the map and answer the following questions, giving the right directions or asking for the right ones.*

Example: Mi scusi, dov'è la stazione dei treni? *Excuse me, where is the train station?*

- Deve andare sempre dritto..... *You must go straight on.*

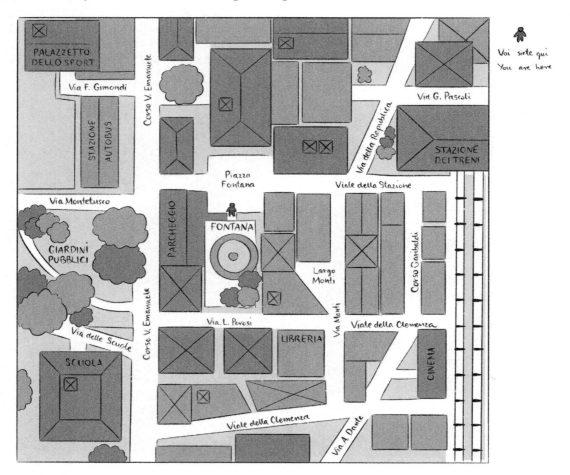

- **Mi scusi, dov'è la scuola?** *Excuse me, where is the school?*

___

Deve andare a sinistra, sempre dritto. È vicino al palazzetto dello sport. *You must go to the left, then straight on. It is near the sports hall.*

- **Mi scusi, dov'è il cinema?** *Excuse me, where is the cinema?*

___

- **Mi scusi, dov'è la libreria?** *Excuse me, where is the library?*

___

IL TEMPO
THE WEATHER

There is something you should be aware of. Italians love talking—and mostly complaining—about the weather! And this is not something you would discuss only when in the elevator with a stranger. It is actually a very common topic even when talking to friends, family and colleagues.

If you are willing to make some Italian friends, or maybe you just want to talk a little with some locals or check the weather forecasts on TV, then you need to learn the vocabulary related to the weather!

First things first: How should you **ask what the weather is like** in Italian? There are two ways to ask for this information:

- **Che tempo fa oggi?**
- **Com'è il tempo oggi?**

These are the most common questions people would ask about the weather that day. However, as you might guess, people will more likely ask about the weather expected for the weekend!

Che tempo fa questo fine settimana? *What is the weather like this weekend?*

As you might have noticed, in order to ask about the weather, in Italian we use the verb *fare*, which corresponds to the English *to do* or *to make*.

When you answer that question, though, people rarely use the same verb. You can use it just in some instances—as shown below—but in most cases, you will use the verb *to be* just like in English.

Now that you know how to ask, let's see the possible answers you can give.

fa caldo / è caldo

it is hot

fa freddo / è freddo

it is cold

è soleggiato / c'è il sole

it is sunny

piove

it is raining

è ventoso / c'è vento

it is windy

nevica / c'è la neve

it is snowing

è nuvoloso

it is cloudy

c'è la tempesta

it is stormy

Finally, yet importantly since we are talking about the weather, it is definitely useful to learn the **names of the seasons** as well!

primavera = *spring*

estate = *summer*

autunno = *autumn*

inverno = *winter*

1) Il meteo. *Look at the weather forecast and describe the weather in Italy. Please use al nord (in the north), al sud (in the south), ad est (to the east) and ad ovest (west) to describe the different situations.*

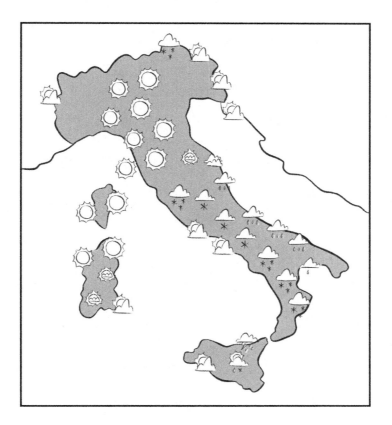

_____

_____

_____

2) Che tempo fa oggi? *What is the weather like today in your city? Describe it in Italian using the vocabulary you have just learned.*

_____

_____

_____

FARE ACQUISTI
SHOPPING

When traveling, shopping is always a tempting activity. Whether you are buying souvenirs, clothes or local food, it is always useful to know how to **ask for prices** and all the **vocabulary related to money** and spending it!

First of all, prices should always be clearly visible in a shop; always check for price tags. In addition, you should know that, in Italy, vendors are required by law to issue a receipt after a purchase. If you do not get a receipt, do not hesitate to ask for one.

Mi può dare lo scontrino per favore? *May I have the receipt, please?*

In case of doubt, you should always ask for prices before going to the register. The key verb to ask for prices is **costare**, to cost, a regular verb belonging to the group of verbs ending with –are.

How can you ask for prices in Italian? As in English, you have two options:

Quanto costa? *How much is it? / How much does it cost?*

Quanto costano? *How much are they? / How much do they cost?*

You use the first question when asking the price for a single object. On the other hand, you use the second question when you ask the price for several items, or when referring to a plural noun.

Examples:

- **Quanto costa l'anello?** *How much is the ring?*
- **Quanto costano le tre cartoline?** *How much are the three postcards?*
- **Quanto costano i pantaloni?** *How much are the pants?*

As you know, the Italian currency is the euro. Please note that, in Italian, euro is both singular and plural, so you do not have to add an extra "s" when making the plural form.

Examples:

- **La calamita costa 1 euro** *The magnet costs 1 euro*
- **Le magliette costano 10 euro l'una** *The T-shirts cost 10 euros each*

And how would you read a price like €15.50, for example?

It is quite easy! You would read it as fifteen euros and fifty, or **quindici euro e cinquanta**.

👍 **Attention!** Of course, when you use the verb costare, do not forget to conjugate it according to the subject of the sentence.

ESERCIZI
EXERCISES XIV

1) Chiedi il prezzo. *Ask for the price of the following items and answer the question according to the price shown.*

· Pizza, 7€

_____ ?

_____

· Gonna *(Skirt)*, 15€

_____ ?

_____

· Calzini *(Socks)*, 3,50€

_____ ?

_____

2) ◀)) Ascolta l'audio. *Listen to the audio file and fill in the blanks with the right words*

_____, come posso aiutarla?

Salve, _____ questo orologio?

_____

Lo trovo un po' _____, ma lo prendo comunque.

Perfetto, possiamo andare alla _____ Mi segua.

Translation:

Good morning, how can I help you?

Hi, how much is this clock?

Fifty euros.

I find it a bit expensive, but I will take it.

Perfect, we can go to the register, then. Please follow me.

MODI DI DIRE
SAYINGS

The end of a chapter means a new section on Italian sayings! As we have done in the previous chapters, some of the following sayings will be related to the topics we have studied in this part of the workbook, like traveling and time.

Would you like to talk like a real native? Let's discover other popular Italian sayings! *Cominciamo!*

Chi tardi arriva male alloggia.

Talking about time and being late! This saying means that whoever shows up late, gets the worst place. It has the same meaning as the English "First come, first served", or "The early bird gets the worm", even if those talk about the advantage of being the first and not the disadvantage of being last.

Chi va piano va sano e va lontano.

This *modo di dire* is very common! It literally means, "Whoever goes slowly, goes healthy and far", meaning that you do not have to rush things.

Tempo al tempo.

Literally translated as "Time to time", in proper English we would say "All in good time", meaning that things will happen when it is time, and sometimes not when you want them to happen.

La gatta frettolosa ha fatto i gattini ciechi.

The literal translation of this *modo di dire* is quite funny, "The hasty cat gave birth to blind kittens". Once again, the meaning of this saying is do not be in a rush, as you will not do a good job. In English, we would say "Haste makes waste".

SECTION 4

SECTION 4 – SPORT E HOBBY
SPORTS AND HOBBIES

For this new chapter, we have decided to focus on **topics related to free time**. Our life is not made just of work—everyone has different interests, passions, things we like to do whenever we can.

You should be able to discuss the things you like doing in Italian as well! That is why, in this chapter, we will give you all the tools you need in order to talk about your favorite sports and hobbies.

Sei pronto a iniziare? *Are you ready to start?*

GLI SPORT
SPORTS

Let's face the truth: people just love sports. Maybe someone prefers to practice them, while others enjoy watching them on TV, and other people love doing both things!

The most common sport in Italy is probably football (soccer, but let's keep it as *football* for international purposes)—*il calcio*—which most children practice, and most adults watch on TV—or maybe play once a week with their old friends.

Below you will find a table with the most popular sports in Italy and everything you need to practice them.

Sport	Cosa Serve
	Things You Need
Calcio *Football*	**Palla** *Ball* – **Campo da calcio** *Football field*
Calcetto *Five-a-side Football*	**Palla**
Pallavolo *Volleyball*	**Palla** – **Rete** *Net*
Basket *Basketball*	**Palla** – **Canestro** *Hoop*
Tennis *Tennis*	**Pallina** *Tennis ball* – **Racchetta** *Racket*
Nuoto *Swimming*	**Piscina** *Swimming pool* - **Costume** *Swimsuit*
Danza *Dance*	**Scarpette da danza** *Ballet shoes*
Pallamano *Handball*	**Palla**
Pallanuoto *Water polo*	**Piscina** - *Palla*
Golf	**Mazze da golf** *Golf clubs* – **Campi da golf** *Gold course* - **Pallina**
Equitazione *Horseback riding*	**Cavallo** *Horse* – **Sella** *Saddle*
Ciclismo *Cycling*	**Bicicletta** *Bike* – **Casco** *Helmet*
Ginnastica *Gymnastics*	**Palestra** *Gym*

As for the verb you should use in order to tell someone which sport you practice, in Italian you should use the irregular verb **fare**—*to do*. In English, we mainly use the verb "to play" when talking about sports, whose translation in Italian is "*giocare*". You can use **giocare**, but, in this instance, you must not forget the preposition "**a**" right after the verb.

However, as in English, you cannot use *giocare* for all sports. For example, you do not say *I play cycling*—in this instance, your only option is to use the verb *fare*.

Examples:

- **Faccio** pallavolo / **Gioco a** pallavolo – *I play volleyball*
- **Fanno** ciclismo – *They do cycling*

ESERCIZI
EXERCISES I

1) Rispondi alle domande. *Answer the following questions.*

- **Che sport pratichi?** *Which sport do you play?*

_____

- **Quando pratichi il tuo sport?** *When do you practice your sport?*

_____

- **Quali sport ti piace guardare alla TV?** *Which sports do you like watching on TV?*

_____

- **Cosa ti serve per praticare il tuo sport?** *What do you need in order to practice your sport?*

_____

2) Giocare o fare? *Which verb(s) can you use to talk about the following sports? Put an X in the table below.*

Sport	Giocare (a)	Fare
Calcio		
Golf		
Equitazione		
Pallavolo		
Danza		
Ciclismo		
Pallamano		
Nuoto		

GLI HOBBY
HOBBIES

When it comes to the world of hobbies, we have endless possibilities. Everyone enjoys different things/activities, and this is why discovering someone's hobbies can be so interesting. You never stop learning something new!

If you want to ask someone what he/she likes doing as a hobby, the question you should ask is:

Che hobby hai? *What hobbies do you have?*

In the following sections, we will learn how to talk in a more comprehensive way about hobbies and sports—for example, how you can compare things—but for now, let's take a look at a list of the most common hobbies people enjoy in their free time.

- **fare sport** = *to do sports*
- **andare in palestra** = *to go to the gym*
- **guardare la TV** = *to watch TV*
- **fare giardinaggio** = *gardening*
- **collezionismo (francobolli, monete, miniature...)** = *collecting (stamps, coins, miniatures...)*
- **fare trekking** = *to hike*
- **cucinare** = *to cook*
- **leggere** = *to read*
- **scrivere** = *to write*
- **disegnare** = *to draw*
- **dipingere** = *to paint*
- **fotografia** = *photography*

👍 (Please note that, in Italian, you do not say "to take pictures", but "to do pictures", fare fotografie)

- **fare bricolage** = *DIY*
- **fare volontariato** = *to volunteer*
- **giocare online** = *to play online games*
- **giocare ai videogiochi** = *to play videogames*

If someone asks you **Che hobby hai?**, you can answer just with your hobbies or, as in English, you can give a full answer by saying **Mi piace...** (*I like...*).

The use of the verb *to like* in Italian—**piacere**—is a bit peculiar. Let's look at its conjugation.

Piacere *(To like)*

Mi piace / piacciono

Ti piace / piacciono

Gli / Le piace / piacciono

Ci piace / piacciono

Vi piace / piacciono

A loro piace / piacciono

It looks quite confusing, right? Do not worry, it is easier than it seems! Let's get into the details.

As you might have noticed, you do not have any subject pronouns—*io, tu, lui/lei* etc. The first words that you see are **personal pronouns expressing the person who likes something**. This means that you must *not* say *Io mi piace, Tu ti piace* etc., but just *mi piace, ti piace* etc.

What is the difference between **gli** *piace* and **le** *piace*, then? *Gli* refers to a masculine subject (*lui*), while *le* refers to a feminine one (*lei*).

Examples:

- **Gli** piace il basket = **He** *likes basketball*
- **Le** piace il golf = **She** *likes golf*

Finally, what is the difference between **piace** and **piacciono**? It is very easy. You use *piace*, when someone likes just one thing—or the noun that follows is singular or it is a verb—while you use *piacciono* when there are more things that someone likes, or when the word that follows is plural.

Examples:

- A loro **piace** lo sport = *They like sport*
- Ci **piacciono** le partite di calcio = *We like football matches*
- Mi **piace** guardare la TV = *I like watching TV*

In English, when a verb follows the verb to like, you need to use its -ing form—I like hik<u>ing</u>, for example. In Italian, you have to use the base form of that verb, so its infinitive with the classic –are, -ere or –ire ending.

Examples:

- Gli piace **mangiare** = *He likes **eating***
- Ci piace **fare** fotografie = *We like **taking** pictures*

Of course, if you want to say that you do *not* like something, the only thing you need to do is to add **"non"** before the personal pronoun. The only exception is for the subject pronoun they, as you will place *non* between *a loro* and *piace* or *piacciono*.

Examples:

- **Non** mi piace ballare = *I do not like dancing*
- A loro **non** piace cucinare = *They do not like cooking*

ESERCIZI
EXERCISES II

1) Rispondi alle domande. *Answer the following questions:*

- **Che hobby hai?** *What's your hobby?*

  _____

- **Che cosa ti piace fare nel fine settimana?** *What do you like doing on the weekend?*

  _____

- **Che cosa piace fare al tuo migliore amico?** *What does your best friend like doing?*

  _____

2) Metti una X. *Put an X in the table below to indicate whether you like those hobbies (mi piace) or not (non mi piace).*

Hobby	Mi piace	Non mi piace
Cucinare		
Giardinaggio		
Collezionare francobolli		
Fare trekking		
Leggere		
Fare bricolage		
Fare sport		
Disegnare		

IL COMPARATIVO
THE COMPARATIVE

We compare things all the time, without even realizing it. This is why knowing how to **make a comparison in Italian** is so important. And we want to give you all the tools you need in order to feel comfortable while speaking this new language.

There are three types of comparison: **positive, negative, and of equality.**

In English, with a positive or negative comparison, you use the comparative adjective—colder, more expensive or less interesting, for example—followed by "than" and the second term of comparison. It might seem obvious, but of course, in order to make a comparison you need two terms of comparison.

Example: *My house is warmer than yours*, where "my house" is the first term of comparison, "warmer" is the comparative adjective, and "yours"—so your house—is the second term of comparison.

With a comparison of equality, you still have the two terms of comparison, but they are on the same level.

Example: *My pullover is as warm as your coat*, meaning that the pullover—the first term of comparison—and the coat—the second one—are equally warm.

After this short overview of the different types of comparatives in English, let's now see how to use them in Italian.

Comparativo di Maggioranza
Positive Comparative

Good news! For once, we have something that is actually easier than in English. If in English we have two options to make the positive comparative—i.e., adding the suffix "–er" or "more" in front of the adjective—in Italian there is only one way to do it.

You just need to add *più* in front of the comparative adjective.

For example, **più caldo** means **warmer**.

How should we introduce the second term of comparison, then? The English *"than"*, which follows the comparative adjective, is the Italian preposition *"di"*. We think you know what is coming next.

If there is an article after *di*, introducing the second term of comparison, *di* and the article will merge and create an articled preposition. If you still have some doubts about articled prepositions, we invite you to review them in the corresponding section of this workbook.

Examples:

- La mia casa è **più** grande **dell'**appartamento *(My house is bigger than the apartment)*. You have **dell'** as **di** merged with **l'**, which is the article for the noun *appartamento*.

- Il computer è **più** lento **del** tablet *(The computer is slower than the tablet)*.

You have **del** as **di** merged with **il**, which is the article for the noun tablet.

However, some adjectives have both a regular form of positive comparative and an irregular one. Let's discover them in the table below.

Adjective	Comparatives
Buono *Good*	**Più buono** or **migliore** *Better*
Cattivo *Bad*	**Più cattivo** or **peggiore** *Worse*
Grande *Big*	**Più grande** or **maggiore** *Bigger*
Piccolo *Small*	**Più piccolo** or **minore** *Smaller*

Since **migliore**, **peggiore**, **maggiore** and **minore** are already comparative, they do **not** need to be preceded by **"più"**.

Here are some helpful examples to get familiar with the *positive comparative*:

- Laura è **più intelligente** di me. *Laura is smarter than me.*

- Tuo fratello è **più alto** di te. *Your brother is taller than you.*

- La pasta è **più buona** della pizza. *Pasta is better than pizza.*

- La tua intonazione è **migliore** della mia. *Your intonation is better than mine.*

Please note that, with regard to the adjectives **buono** and **cattivo**, generally the choice of the comparative is based on the context: if the adjective refers to the *moral characteristic of a person* or to the *feature of a physical object* we use "più buono/più cattivo", while if it is referred to a *skill* or to an *abstract concept* we use "migliore/peggiore".

Comparativo di Minoranza

Negative Comparative

Of course, in this instance, we won't say that something is "more" than something else, but the opposite.

In English, when we make a negative comparison, we use "less" in front of the comparative adjective, followed by "than" and the second term of comparison.

In Italian, in order to make a negative comparison, you just need to replace that "less" with its translation—**meno** - followed by the comparative adjective and, once again, the preposition **"di"**.

As we have seen for the positive comparative, if the preposition *di* is followed by the article of the second term of comparison, you will get an articled preposition.

Examples:

- Il film è **meno** interessante **del** libro. *The movie is less interesting than the book.*

You have *del* as *di* merged with *il*, which is the article for the noun *libro*.

- Sono **meno** alta **di** tua sorella. *I am less tall than your sister.*

In this instance, we do not have any articled preposition. If you remember, when we discussed the possessive adjectives, we said that the possessives related to family members in their singular form do not require an article.

Comparativo di Uguaglianza
Comparative of Equality

As expected, when we make a comparison of equality, we still have two terms of comparison but they are on the same level.

In English, we do it by using "as.... as", with the comparative adjective between them and the second term of comparison right after the second "as".

Example: My brother is as smart as I am.

In Italian, it is kind of the same mechanism. Our Italian "as…as" is **"tanto… quanto"**, with the comparative adjective between those two words and the second term of comparison right after *quanto*.

In this instance, then, since there is no preposition involved, we won't have any articled prepositions.

Examples:

- La mia borsa è **tanto** grande **quanto** il tuo zaino. *My bag is as big as your backpack.*
- Il leone corre **tanto** veloce **quanto** la tigre. *The lion run as fast as the tiger.*

To close this section, we will list a few adjectives that might be useful to make some comparisons:

grande/i = *big*

piccolo/a/i/e = *small*

alto/a/i/e = *tall*

basso/a/i/e = *short*

bello/a/i/e = *beautiful*

brutto/a/i/e = *ugly*

interessante/i = *interesting*

noioso/a/i/e = *boring*

divertente/i = *funny*

intelligente/i = *smart*

We remind you that, when you see four different options, they refer to the masculine singular, feminine singular, masculine plural and feminine plural form of the same adjective. When you see only two, it means that you only have one option for the singular form—masculine and feminine—and one for the plural—masculine and feminine.

ESERCIZI
EXERCISES III

1) Traduzione. *Translate the following sentences into Italian.*

- Giulio is taller than my cousin:

  _____

- Basketball is less tiring *(faticoso)* than volleyball:

  _____

- Books are more interesting than video games:

  _____

- My sister is as fun as her friends:

  _____

- Golf is less dynamic *(dinamico)* than handball:

  _____

2) Il comparativo. *Change the sentence—and the comparative—so that it has the same meaning.*

Example: La mia camera è più ordinata della tua. *My room is tidier than yours* =

La tua camera è meno ordinata della mia.

- Questo fiore è più bello della pianta *(This flower is more beautiful than the plant)* =

  _____

- I gatti sono più furbi dei cani *(Cats are more clever than dogs)* =

  _____

- La lezione di storia è meno noiosa di quella di matematica *(The history lesson is less boring than the math one)* =

  _____

- Il quaderno è meno colorato del libro *(The notebook is less colorful than the book)* =

  _____

IL SUPERLATIVO
THE SUPERLATIVE

After working on the different types of Italian comparatives, we must learn how to **make a superlative** as well!

In English, the superlative is marked by the use of "the" + the adjective with the suffix -*est*—for example, the smallest—or "the" followed by "most" and the adjective itself—for example, the most beautiful.

Examples:

- My house is *the tallest* building in the city.

- That scarf is *the most expensive* item in this shop.

In Italian, we have two superlatives, **superlativo relativo** and **superlativo assoluto**, that we will discuss right away.

What are these two kinds of superlatives, and how can you tell the difference?

Superlativo relativo
Relative Superlative

In Italian, the difference between **superlativo relativo** and **superlativo assoluto** is self-evident because they are very different in the way they are structured.

In order to have a superlativo relativo, you need the following structure of the superlative:

Articolo determinativo + più/meno + aggettivo+ di/che/tra

The first thing you need is the **articolo determinativo—il, lo, la** etc.—which, of course, will have to match the gender and the number of the subject of the sentence.

Then you have to use **"più"**—more—or **"meno"**—less—that you will pick according to what you want to say. We have already seen these words in the previous section about comparatives.

The third element is the **adjective**, and the final one will be the **prepositions di** (of) or **tra** (between/among) or the **conjunction che** (that).

It might seem complicated; trust us, it is not. With some practical examples, it will become clearer!

Examples:

- Il mio cane è **il più divertente del** quartiere. *(My dog is the funniest of the neighborhood.)*
- Questa strada è **la più veloce tra** quelle della città. *(This street is the fastest among those in the city.)*
- È **la serie TV più bella che** io abbia mai visto. *(It is the most beautiful TV series that I have ever seen.)*

As you might have noticed, the main feature of this superlative is the fact that we actually have a comparison. In our examples, the second terms of comparison would be the dogs in that neighborhood, the streets of that city, and all the other TV series I have seen before.

What really changes from a simple comparative is the presence of the articolo determinativo.

Examples:

- **Comparative:** Le mie scarpe sono più costose di quelle dei miei amici (My shoes are more expensive than my friends' shoes.)
- **Superlative:** Le mie scarpe sono **le** più costose tra quelle dei miei amici (My shoes are the most expensive among my friends' shoes.)

Superlativo assoluto
Absolute Superlative

At first glance, the difference between a comparative and a superlativo relativo might not seem immediately obvious, but you will never doubt the difference between a superlativo relativo and a superlativo assoluto.

First difference: When we use the superlativo assoluto, **there is no second term of comparison**. For example, if I say "I am the shortest", I am using a superlativo assoluto as I'm not providing any other information. I am just the shortest, but people do not know if I am talking in general terms, if I am referring to my family members, etc.

The second difference concerns how to create a superlativo assoluto. This is how you structure it:

Adjective + the suffix **-issimo, -issima, -issimi, -issime**

Why do we have four different suffixes? You have probably already guessed the answer. You will pick –*issimo* for masculine singular nouns, -*issima* for feminine singular ones, -*issimi* for masculine plural nouns, and –*issime* for feminine plural ones.

Examples:

- Mia sorella è **divertentissima**. *(My sister is the funniest.)*
  In this instance, the base form of the adjective is *divertente*—fun—that becomes *divertentissima* as soon as we add the suffix *–issima*. We picked *–issima* as the subject is a feminine noun—*sorella*.

- I tuoi libri sono **noiosissimi.** *(Your books are the most boring.)*
  In this instance, the base form of the adjective is *noioso*—boring—that becomes *noiosissimi* as it refers to a masculine plural noun—*libri*.

- Il vostro letto è **comodissimo.** *(Your bed is the most confortable.)*
  In this instance, the base form of the adjective is *comodo*—comfortable—that becomes *comodissimo* as it refers to a masculine singular noun – *letto*.

One last thing. As we have seen while studying the comparative, there are some adjectives with both a **regular** form of comparative and an **irregular** one. The same applies for their superlativo assoluto.

Aggettivo	Superlativo assoluto
Buono *Good*	**Buonissimo** or **ottimo** *The best*
Cattivo *Bad*	**Cattivissimo** or **pessimo** *The worst*
Grande *Big*	**Grandissimo**, or **massimo** *The biggest*
Piccolo *Small*	**Piccolissimo** or **minimo** *The smallest*

Is everything clear now? Let's have some fun with superlatives, then!

ESERCIZI
EXERCISES IV

1) Superlativo Relativo (SR) or Superlativo Assoluto (SA)? *Write the abbreviation next to the following sentences.*

- Il mio giardino è il più grande delle case qui intorno *(My garden is the biggest among those of the houses around here.)* _____

- Questa macchina è velocissima *(This car is the fastest.)* _____

- Tra le persone qui presenti, sono la più stanca *(Among the people here, I'm the most tired.)* _____

- Le margherite sono bellissime a primavera *(Daisies are the most beautiful in spring.)* _____

- Il mio zaino è il più pesante della classe *(My backpack is the heaviest one in the class.)* _____

2) Scrivi la frase. *Write the following sentences with the right superlativo relativo or superlativo assoluto.*
Remember to adapt the adjective so that it matches the gender and number of the subject.
Example: Io / sono / intelligente __ Io sono intelligentissimo__ *I am the smartest.*

- La tartaruga / è / lento / degli animali *(The turtle is the slowest animal.)*
  _____

- I miei zii / sono / gentile (My uncles are the kindest.)
  _____

- Le stelle / sono / grande (The stars are huge.)
  _____

- Voi / siete / alto / della famiglia (You are the tallest ones in the family.)
  _____

AVVERBI DI FREQUENZA
ADVERBS OF FREQUENCY

This section of the chapter will be dedicated to adverbs of frequency. Maybe you are wondering what they are, if you have already used them, etc. Actually, you probably use them on a daily basis!

As their name suggests, adverbs of frequency express **how often a certain thing is done**. In English, we have six main adverbs of frequency. Please look at them in the table below along with their Italian translation.

Always	**Sempre**
Often	**Spesso**
Usually	**Di solito/solitamente**
Sometimes	**A volte**
Rarely	**Di rado/raramente**
Never	**Mai**

Now you realized why adverbs of frequency are so important! We use them all the time to discuss all sorts of things.

Let's discuss their position within a sentence. In English, we place the adverb of frequency between the subject pronoun and the verb. Exception: when there is the verb to be, the adverb of frequency come after the verb.

Examples:

·   I *always* go to the swimming pool on Sundays.

·   They *sometimes* play tennis.

·   She is *never* satisfied with her work.

Alternatively, when a verb is conjugated in the present perfect tense—have/has + past participle of the verb—the adverb of frequency goes between the auxiliary verb—to have—and the past participle.

Examples:

·   You have *never* worked on that task.

·   We have *often* traveled in Europe.

In Italian—for once!—we are more flexible, meaning that **there is not a fixed position for the adverbs of frequency**. In general, you can find them after the verb and, when it is in the past tense, between the auxiliary verb—to be or to have—and the past participle (we will discuss the past tense in the next section, do not worry!).

Examples:

- Dico **sempre** a mia mamma di comprare la cioccolata (*I always tell my mom to buy some chocolate.*)

- Ha **spesso** mangiato a quel ristorante (*He/She has often eaten in that restaurant.*)

However, if we take into account the second example, we could have placed "*spesso*" at the end of the sentence - *Ha mangiato a quel ristorante spesso* - and the meaning would be the same.

In certain instances, we can place the adverb of frequency at the beginning of the sentence as well.

Examples:

- **A volte**, vado al supermercato la sera (*I sometimes go to the supermarket in the evening*). I could have said "*Vado al supermercato la sera a volte*" as well.

- **Di solito** pranziamo tardi (*We usually have a late lunch*). I could have said "*Pranziamo tardi di solito*" as well.

👍 **Attention!** In Italian, we can have **double negatives**, which are sentences with two negative forms. In English, double negatives cannot be used.

For example, you cannot say "I have *not never* worked in my life", but you just use one negative form by saying "I have *never* worked in my life". In English, then, the adverb of frequency "never" is the central element of that negative sentence.

In Italian, it is quite the opposite. You must make a double negative for your negative sentence with the adverb of frequency "never" to make sense.

For example, you cannot say "*Hanno **mai** studiato*" (*They have never studied*), as it makes no sense. You have to say "***Non** hanno **mai** studiato*", with a double negative sentence where the two negative forms are represented by "***non***" and "***mai***".

ESERCIZI
EXERCISES V

1) Collega gli avverbi. *Link the adverb of frequency in English with the corresponding Italian one.*

Never	Solitamente
Sometimes	Sempre
Often	Raramente
Always	Spesso
Rarely	A volte
Usually	Mai

2) Le tue abitudini. *In Italian, write some activities that you always – sometimes – often – rarely – usually do.*

Durante la settimana *During the week*
Sempre:
Di solito:
Spesso:
A volte:
Raramente:
Mai:
Durante il fine settimana *During the weekend*
Sempre:
Di solito:
Spesso:
A volte:
Raramente:
Mai:

FARE DEI PIANI
MAKING PLANS

Now you know how to tell the time, to express how often you do several things, and how to translate hobbies and sports. It is time to **make some plans in Italian**!

Whether you want to schedule an appointment for work, or just meet up with some Italian friends, knowing how to make plans in Italian will surely help you.

In order to show you how it works, please look at the following dialogues. Specifically, the first one is about scheduling a business appointment—*un appuntamento di lavoro*—and the other one is about meeting up with a friend—*incontrare un amico*.

We will discuss their features right after each dialogue!

Dialogo 1

Tu: Buongiorno Vittorio! Come sta oggi?

Capo: Buongiorno! Sto bene, grazie. E Lei?

Tu: Tutto bene. Che ne dice di pranzare insieme oggi? È libero?

Capo: Certo, con piacere. A che ora?

Tu: All'una?

Capo: Perfetto. Ci troviamo davanti al bar, ok?

Tu: Benissimo, a dopo!

Translation

You: Good morning, Vittorio! How are you today?

***Boss**: Good morning! I am fine, thank you. And you?*

You: I am good. What about having lunch together today? Are you free?

***Boss**: Of course, I would love to. What time?*

You: At 1 p.m.?

***Boss**: Perfect. Let's meet up in front of the café, okay?*

You: All right, see you later!

This is our first situation. You are talking to your boss, and it is likely that you are going to be **more formal** with him, meaning that, in Italian, you will have to use the courtesy form—the subject pronoun she, *lei*.

Please note that in Italy it is not that common to have lunch with your boss. Of course, it all depends on the company you are working for and your boss's personality, but we cannot say that it is a common practice.

Dialogo 2

Amico: Ciao, da quanto tempo! Come te la passi?

Tu: Non mi lamento! E tu?

Amico: Tutto bene. Che ne dici di andare a prendere un caffè uno di questi giorni?

Tu: Volentieri! Sono libero martedì e giovedì mattina.

Amico: Preferisco il giovedì mattina. Alle 10?

Tu: Perfetto. Dove ci troviamo?

Amico: Alla pasticceria vicino al cinema, se per te va bene. I dolci sono ottimi!

Tu: Certo! A giovedì allora!

Amico: A giovedì, buona serata!

Translation

Friend: *Hi, long time no see! How are you doing?*

You: I cannot complain! How about you?

Friend: *I am good. Would you like to grab a coffee one of these days?*

You: I would love to. I am free on Tuesday and Thursday morning.

Friend: *I would prefer on Thursday morning. At 10 a.m.?*

You: Perfect. Where shall we meet?

Friend: *At the bakery near the cinema, if it is okay for you. Their cakes are delicious!*

You: Of course! See you on Thursday, then!

Friend: *See you on Thursday, have a nice evening!*

In this second situation, you are talking to an old friend of yours. The language is **not formal at all**, and indeed, it gives us the chance to explore some words that are quite commonly used when talking to a friend or someone you are familiar with.

You probably noticed the first question, **Come te la passi?** It could be translated as "How are you doing?", and you should use this question only with people you know pretty well.

👍 **Useful tip:** If you have an Italian friend and you want to meet up with him/her to have breakfast, lunch or dinner, and you do not want him/her to look at you as if you were an alien from another planet, when should you ask him/her to meet?

Colazione: anytime from 9 until 10:30/11 (unless you have to go to work)

Pranzo: not before 12:30! In general, Italians eat around 1-1:30 p.m.

Cena: not before 8pm! Unless you are planning to have an **aperitivo**—a happy hour. In that instance, people usually meet around 7p.m.

 **ESERCIZI**
EXERCISES VI

1) Scrivi un messaggio. *Write a text to your friend Marco. You will ask him to meet at 8:30 p.m. to have dinner together at your place. Tell him your address and explain to him how to get to your place (review the section on how to give directions if needed!)*

2) Scrivi un'email. *Write an email to your professor at the university. Tell him that you would like to attend (frequentare) his course, but that you are not available on Fridays. Ask him if that is a problem, and if you can meet in his office (ufficio) to discuss the program (programma) of the course. Ask him when he is available (days and time of day).*

MODI DI DIRE
SAYINGS

Let's close this new chapter with our usual section on Italian sayings. We hope that you are enjoying this immersion into Italian culture as much as we are enjoying sharing everything we know with you.

Andiamo! *Let's go!*

A caval donato non si guarda in bocca.

This *modo di dire* is translated as "Don't look a gift horse in the mouth". At the beginning, it might seem quite weird as an expression, but it actually means that you should not question the value of a gift. If you receive one, you should not complain about it, judge it, or be ungrateful. A gift is a gift, after all!

A buon intenditore poche parole.

This saying comes from the corresponding one in ancient Latin, *Intelligenti pauca*. It means that someone smart does not need many words in order to understand. In English, it could be translated as "A word to the wise".

Il lupo perde il pelo ma non il vizio.

The sentence literally means "The wolf loses his hairs, but not his vice". In proper English, we would translate it as "Old habits die hard", meaning that it is quite unlikely, if not impossible, that someone can really change his old (questionable) habits, *il vizio*.

Ride bene chi ride ultimo!

If someone tells you this sentence, well, you are in trouble! It is a kind of warning. We would translate it as "He who laughs last laughs best!", and it means that you should not celebrate something until it is finally over, because the outcome can completely change—and not in your favor.

SECTION 5

SECTION 5 - PARLARE AL PASSATO
TALKING IN THE PAST TENSE

Are you ready to take a BIG step in your knowledge of the Italian language?

Yes! Now that we know how to discuss things in the present tense, we will move forward and learn **how to build the past tense in Italian**. Specifically, for now, we will focus on one of the past tenses as—sorry to give you some bad news—there are several past tenses in Italian.

IL PASSATO PROSSIMO
SIMPLE PAST

Fear not: you will soon discover that the past tense we are working on—the so-called **passato prossimo**—looks like an English tense you are already familiar with.

We are talking about *present perfect*. Just to refresh your memory, an example of a sentence with present perfect could be "I have studied at public schools". In order to create this tense, you need to use the auxiliary verb *to have* + *the past participle* of the main verb.

Examples:

· We *have traveled* all over the world

· She *has worked* as a nurse for 22 years

· They *have never been* to Australia

Well, our *passato prossimo* shares with the present perfect its main structure. In order to create a passato prossimo, we need the *auxiliary verb* to have or to be—more on this later—and the *past participle* of the main verb.

What is different from the present perfect, though, is its use. In English, present perfect is a tense between past and present, expressing a generic action/situation or something that began in the past but still goes on.

❶ Fear not: you will soon discover that the past tense we are working on—the so-called *passato prossimo*—looks like an English tense you are already familiar with.

We are talking about *present perfect*. Just to refresh your memory, an example of a sentence with present perfect could be "I have studied at public schools". In order to create this tense, you need to use the auxiliary verb *to have* + *the past participle* of the main verb.

What is different from the present perfect, though, is its use. In English, present perfect is a tense between past and present, expressing a generic action/situation or something that began in the past but still goes on.

In terms of use, the passato prossimo corresponds to the English simple past—I studied, I ate, I went, etc. This means that we will **use the passato prossimo to express an action that began in the past, but is now over**.

Examples:

- **Ho imparato l'italiano a 16 anni.** *I learned Italian when I was 16.*
- **Abbiamo visitato la Spagna l'anno scorso.** *We visited Spain last year.*
- **Hanno visto un film sabato sera.** *They watched a movie on Saturday night.*

As you can see from the examples above, all these actions/events began and finished in the past.

Let's take a closer look at the examples in order to better explain this concept: you learned Italian when you were 16, but you are not 16 anymore. You visited Spain last year, but then you came back home. They watched a movie on Saturday night, but now it is a different day and they are doing something different.

Whenever you use simple past in English, you will use the passato prossimo in Italian.

Now, let's start with the first element of its structure: **the auxiliary verb**. As mentioned earlier, in Italian we can use to be or to have.

But when should you pick to have rather than to be?

It is actually quite easy. Most verbs will take the verb to have as an auxiliary verb. The verbs requiring to be as the auxiliary are the following ones:

- The verb **to be** itself!

- Some **intransitive verbs**, i.e., verbs which do not take a direct object, like accadere *(to happen)*, stare *(to stay)*, morire *(to die)*, andare *(to go)*, venire *(to come)*, partire *(to leave)*, cadere *(to fall)*, arrivare *(to arrive)*.

- **Reflexive verbs**, like prepararsi *(to get ready)*, lavarsi *(to wash yourself)*, pentirsi *(to regret)*.

All the other verbs will need to have. We invite you to review the conjugation of *essere* and *avere* if you have some doubts!

Then, second element: Il *participio passato*, the past participle. In English, you can make a past participle by adding the suffix -*ed* for regular verbs—for example, played, studied, cooked etc. —or by using a specific form of the verb for the *irregular ones*, for example, done, made, thought etc.

In Italian, in order to **make a participio passato**, you can follow these schematic rules:

1. Verbs of the 1st group **(-are)**: verb root + the suffix **-ato**

Examples: mangi**are** *(to eat)* ➜ mangi**ato** *(eaten)*

Other verbs: parlato *(spoken)*, andato *(gone)* etc.

2. Verbs of the 2nd group **(-ere)**: verb root + the suffix **-uto**

Examples: cred**ere** (to believe) ➜ cred**uto** (believed)

Other verbs: venduto *(sold)*, caduto *(fallen)*, avuto *(had)* etc.

3. Verbs of the 3rd group **(-ire)**: verb root + the suffix **-ito**

Examples: cap**ire** *(to understand)* ➜ cap**ito** *(understood)*

Other verbs: sentito *(heard)*, partito *(left)*, costruito *(built)* etc.

Unfortunately, as in English, we have some **irregular past participles** as well, and they mainly belong to the 2nd group, or the verbs ending with –ere. You will find a list of some of the most common irregular past participles at the end of this workbook.

When in doubt, look at the list and check if the past participle you are looking for is an irregular one! Do not get scared: We know, it is a long list—and it is not even a comprehensive one! Our suggestion is to learn 3-5 past participles a time. It will not require much time and it is very effective!

Now, let's see an example of conjugation in the passato prossimo tense with the auxiliary verb **to have**.

Passato prossimo di mangiare
Simple past of to eat

Io ho mangiato

Tu hai mangiato

Lui/lei ha mangiato

Noi abbiamo mangiato

Voi avete mangiato

Loro hanno mangiato

As you can see, the only thing you should do is conjugate the verb to have in the present tense. The past participle NEVER changes!

However, what happens when we conjugate a verb requiring the auxiliary to be?

Passato prossimo di andare
Simple past of to go

Io sono andato/a

Tu sei andato/a

Lui è andato / Lei è andata

Noi siamo andati/e

Voi siete andati/e

Loro sono andati/e

In this instance, the first thing you have to do is conjugate the verb "to be" in the present tense. Then, as you will notice from the example, you need to adapt the past participle according to the subject it refers to.

But what does that mean?

It is easier than it seems. When we use the auxiliary verb "to be", the past participle needs to match the gender and the number of the subject.

For example, I will say "**Sei andato**" *(you went)* if the subject is masculine and singular. On the other hand, I will say "**Sei andata**" *(you went)*, if the subject is feminine and singular.

The same applies for the plurals as well. I will say "Siamo andati" *(we went)*, if in my group there are only men, or men with some women. I will say "Siamo andate" *(we went)*, if the group I am talking about is made up of women only.

Before closing this section, let's check the translation of some **useful words** related to the use of the past tense:

ieri = *yesterday*

l'altroieri = *the day before yesterday*

il mese scorso = *last month*

la settimana scorsa = *last week*

l'anno scorso = *last year*

due settimane fa = *two weeks ago*

tre anni fa = *three years ago*

un paio di giorni fa = *a couple of days ago*

When you would use "last" in English, you will have to use **scorso** or **scorsa** in Italian, which goes after the noun it refers to, and does not precede it. You will use **scorso** or **scorsi**—its plural form - for **giorno/i, mese/i or anno/i** as they are masculine nouns.

On the other hand, you will use **scorsa/e** for **settimana/e**, as "week" is a feminine noun in Italian.

If you want to use *"ago"*, then in Italian it will be **fa**. This short word never changes and, as in English, goes right after the word it refers to.

Example: Sette giorni fa. *Seven days ago.*

This is it, we promise! We know that it has been a long section, and that at first, the Italian passato prossimo might seem quite complicated, but it is all a matter of practice, trust us!

Let's start practicing, then!

ESERCIZI
EXERCISES I

1) Essere o avere? *To be (essere) or to have (avere) as the auxiliary verb? Put an X in the table below.*

	Essere	Avere
Andare *to go*		
Prendere *to take*		
Partire *to leave*		
Accendere *to switch on*		
Credere *to believe*		
Succedere *to happen*		
Vestirsi *to get dressed*		
Vedere *to see*		
Cadere *to fall*		

2) Traduzione. *Translate the following verbs into Italian. Please note that there may be some irregular past participles.*

Example: We ate *(mangiare)* = ___Abbiamo mangiato___

- You went *(andare)* = _____

- I was *(essere)* = _____

- They had *(avere)* = _____

- She took *(prendere)* = _____

- We hoped *(sperare)* = _____

- You created *(creare)* = _____

- He left *(partire)* = _____

- I tried *(provare)* = _____

3) 🔊 **Ascolta l'audio.** *Listen to the audio file and fill in the blanks with the right words.*

Ieri _____ al cinema con i miei amici e _____ un film molto divertente. _____ dei popcorn e _____ davanti allo schermo. Alla fine del film, _____ per comprare un panino. alle 22, _____ di fame! Poi _____ a casa.

Translation:

Yesterday, I went to the cinema with my friends and we watched a very funny movie. We bought popcorn and sat in front of the screen. At the end of the movie, we went out to buy a sandwich. We ate at 10 p.m.; I was starving! Then I went back home.

4) Che cosa hai fatto ieri? *What did you do yesterday? Write a short summary of your day using the passato prossimo.*

_____

_____

_____

_____

Example:

Ieri sono stato al mare con un vecchio amico. Siamo partiti alle 9 e siamo arrivati alla spiaggia verso le 10:30. Abbiamo messo gli asciugamani sulla sabbia e ci siamo rilassati. È stata una bella giornata. Abbiamo pranzato in un ristorante sul mare e poi il pomeriggio siamo tornati a casa. La sera sono rimasto sul divano a guardare un film e sono andato a letto verso le 11.

Translation:

Yesterday, I was at the seaside with an old friend of mine. We left at 9 a.m. and we arrived on the beach around 10:30. We put our towels on the sand and relaxed. It was a good day. We had lunch in a restaurant by the sea and we came back home in the afternoon. In the evening, I stayed on the couch watching a movie. I went to bed around 11 p.m.

LA SCUOLA ITALIANA
ITALIAN SCHOOLS

As we discussed simple past in the previous section, we think this would be the perfect time to introduce some **vocabulary about school**—and some cultural information as well.

Perhaps your time in school is a far-off memory, or quite a recent one, or maybe it is your present. In any case, we believe that this section will be interesting, as you will discover some specific things about the Italian school system.

Maybe you are moving to Italy, or thinking about studying in Italy for a semester or a whole year. Or maybe you are just interested in discovering how the Italian school system works.

And here you will find all the answers you need about schools in Italy!

Let's start with the basics, then! As in the US, in Italy there are public and private schools. As you might imagine, public schools are financed by the Italian state, while a private school requires the parents to pay school fees.

The first step of the Italian school is nursery school, or **Asilo nido** in Italian. Children are 0–3 years of age.

Then we have the **Scuola materna**, preschool, for children that are 3–6 years of age. This step is still not compulsory.

From 6 years of age, until 16, we have the so-called **Scuola dell'obbligo**—mandatory school—meaning that all students must attend these school cycles by law.

The **Scuola elementare** lasts 5 years. Originally, there was a final test at the end of primary school, but it has been removed. In primary school, children learn all the basics and start studying a foreign language—or even more than one.

Then you have the **Scuola media**, or lower secondary school, which lasts 3 years. Here, students start to deepen their knowledge. At the end of the third year of school, you have a final exam consisting of written and oral parts.

❶ **Fun fact:** do you know that in Italy students do not have lockers—**armadietti**—in school? Yes, students need to carry everything they need for the classes in their backpacks, every single day.

You can have a backpack filled with books, notebooks and even dictionaries, a musical instrument in one hand—if you have music classes at school—and a big folder for the art lessons in the other one.

When you are 14, you start attending the so-called **Liceo** or **Scuola superiore**, or upper secondary school, which lasts 5 years. In an Italian high school, a student must attend several lessons of different topics according to the type of high school he/she enrolled in.

As an example, you have the "**Liceo linguistico**" (language high school), specialized in foreign languages, the "**Liceo scientifico**", specialized in mathematics and physics, the "**Liceo artistico**", where most subjects are related to art, the "**Liceo classico**", where most teaching is about humanities (history, philosophy etc.) or an "**Istituto tecnico**", a more technical high school.

From primary school to high school, grades are on a scale up to ten, where six is the minimum grade you need to get in order to successfully pass a test.

Here are other fun facts about attending an Italian school.

Do you know that students have "fixed" classes in school? It means that they never change their classes, but it is the teacher going from one class to another in order to teach his/her lessons. And of course, that means that you are stuck with the same classmates for 5 or 3 years!

At the end of the upper secondary school, in order to graduate, you have to take the "terrible" exam most students are worried about—the so-called *Esame di maturità*, that literally means the "Maturity Exam".

This exam consists of written and oral parts—**esami scritti e orali**. The final grade will be given on a scale up to *cento*. A student needs to get a minimum grade of sixty—**sessanta**—to graduate.

And here comes university, *l'***Università**! Of course, university is not mandatory in Italy, even though it is highly recommended, especially if you have attended a more "academic" type of high school and not a "technical" one.

Also, universities are not that expensive in Italy. The fees are calculated according to the family income, and there are several types of facilitation if, for example, you already have a sibling studying at an Italian university.

The Italian system is called *3+2, tre più due*. The so-called **Laurea triennale** is a three-year degree that allows you to enter the world of university graduates.

At the end, students are asked to write a final essay—the *tesi*—that they will discuss in front of a commission of professors. The maximum grade you can get is one hundred and ten and praise—*centodieci e lode*.

Then, students can attend the two-year cycle that follows, the **Laurea magistrale**—Master's degree. Here, students really deepen their education and the subjects they have studied during the first cycle. And, yes, at the end of it you need, once again, to write a *tesi* and discuss it. Exams are endless for real!

While in university, you also have the chance to study abroad—*studiare all'estero*. Thanks to the Erasmus program promoted by the European Union, nowadays more and more Italian students decide to study abroad for a semester or for a whole year. Not only you get the chance to challenge yourself—with a new life, language, school—but you meet people from all over the world, and it truly is an experience that broadens your mind and your perspective.

School system summary:

Asilo nido – Scuola materna – Scuola elementare – Scuola media – Scuola superiore (or liceo) - Università

Let's now discover some useful **vocabulary related to school**:

scuola	=	*school*
materie	=	*subjects*
matematica	=	*math*
letteratura	=	*literature*
geografia	=	*geography*
storia	=	*history*
storia dell'arte	=	*art history*
scienze	=	*science*
chimica	=	*chemistry*
lingua straniera	=	*foreign language*
educazione civica	=	*civic education*
musica	=	*music*
educazione fisica	=	*P.E.*
lezione	=	*lesson*
classe	=	*class/classroom*
verifica	=	*test (in primary and middle school)*
compito in classe	=	*test (in high school)*
esame	=	*exam (in university)*
voto	=	*grade*
interrogazione	=	*oral questions*
compagni di classe	=	*classmates*
maestro	=	*teacher (in primary school)*
professore	=	*professor (from middle school to university)*

👉 **Note:** When addressing a professor, whether you are in middle school, high school or university, the student must use the *courtesy form*, meaning that he/she will talk to the professor using the subject pronoun **Lei.**

Some final information regarding **school hours**.

In general, Italian schools start around 8:30. Depending on the school the student is enrolled in, lessons might end around 1–2 p.m. or there may be some lessons in the afternoon as well. However, some students go to school even on Saturdays, especially when in high school.

The school year begins in September and ends in June, and there is a very good reason for it. Can you imagine having to go to class in the July heat? It would be quite impossible, considering that most Italian schools do not have air conditioning.

Also, spring break does not exist in Italy. When in school, the main holidays students get are for Christmas (a couple of weeks between December and January) and Easter (one week at the end of March or in April).

Then, of course, schools are closed for public holidays like the following:

- **Festa della Liberazione** (April 25th), celebrating the liberation of Italy from the Nazi occupation.
- **Festa dei Lavoratori** (May 1st), corresponding to Labor Day.
- **Festa della Repubblica** (June 2nd), national and Republic day.
- **Ferragosto** (August 15th), Mid-August.
- **Tutti i Santi** (November 1st), All Saints.
- **Immacolata,** (December 8th), Feast of the Immaculate Conception.

This is why, if you are planning to go to Italy, you will probably find out that flights are more expensive around those dates. If you want to save money, it is better to avoid those weeks. You are welcome for the tip!

ESERCIZI
EXERCISES II

1) E la tua scuola? *How is the school system in your country? What are the main pros and cons? Write a short text in Italian.*

_____

_____

_____

_____

_____

_____

2) 🔊 **Ascolta l'audio.** *Listen to the audio file and fill in the blanks with the right words.*

Ho frequentato il _____ nella mia città. _____ quella scuola perché sono sempre stato appassionato alle _____ Ho studiato _____ ma la mia _____ preferita era _____ _____ perché amo leggere. Ho sempre preso _____ e i miei genitori _____ fieri di me quando ho preso il _____

Translation:

I attended the linguistic high school in my city. I chose that school because I have always been fond of foreign languages. I studied English and Russian, but my favorite subject was literature, as I love reading. I have always gotten good grades, and my parents were proud of me when I got my final degree.

MODI DI DIRE
SAYINGS

This is the final section on Italian sayings in our workbook, and we feel like it is the perfect way to close this chapter after having discussed so many things from both a cultural and a grammar point of view!

We hope that you still feel as motivated as you were when you started browsing through the pages of this workbook.

Also, we hope that you are feeling proud about the progress you have made so far! Learning a new language is always challenging, and you are doing such a great job. Keep up the good work!

Now, are you ready to discover the last new *modi di dire*?

Forza! *C'mon!*

Stare con le mani in mano.

We can translate this saying as "To stay with hands in hands", but in English, we would say "To sit on your hands". Of course, when using it, you need to conjugate the verb *stare*. This expression is used to describe someone who is doing nothing while other people are at work, and is a very common *modo di dire* parents use towards their teenagers!

Si chiama Pietro!

People use this saying when lending something. The complete sentence would be "*Si chiama Pietro… Deve tornare indietro!*" - Its name is Pietro… and it has to come back! It is wordplay as "*Pietro*" and "*indietro*" rhyme. This applies to all kinds of objects when you lend them, from a pencil to a car!

Andarsene con la coda tra le gambe.

Literally translated as "To leave with the tail between legs", in English it would be more appropriate to say "To go off with one's tail between one's legs". Of course, when using this saying, you need to conjugate the verb, which is to go, but in this instance it is quite peculiar. In order to help you use this *modo di dire*, here is its conjugation: *Me ne vado, te ne vai, se ne va, ce ne andiamo, ve ne andate, se ne vanno.*

This saying means leaving a situation with shame or embarrassment.

Avere la coda di paglia.

This can be translated as "To have a straw tail", meaning that your tail can easily burst into flames because you have a guilty conscience or maybe because you are wracked with guilt for something you did. When using this saying, you will have to conjugate the verb to have. For example, you would say "*Ha la coda di paglia*" - He/she has a straw tail.

Avere un diavolo per capello.

Our last saying! This one is quite funny as well! It literally means "To have one devil per hair", and unfortunately there is no such saying in English, even if we feel like there should be! It means being enraged, furious, just as if you had a storm of devils on the top of your head!

EXTRA: COMPRENSIONE SCRITTA
READING COMPREHENSION

We have said it a thousand times, and we cannot help but repeat it: in order to learn a new language and start using it with confidence, you need to practice, practice, practice.

That is why we decided to add a bonus exercise at the end of this workbook. Just in case you would like to practice more with something that you have not done so far.

Now that you know tons of vocabulary and grammar, it is time to challenge yourself with your **first reading comprehension**!

Please take your time to listen to the text in order to train your pronunciation. Then, read it aloud and, if you want, you can stop at the end of each sentence and try to translate every word. If you want to check your translation work, or if you have some doubts, you will find the translation of the text at the end of this activity.

At the end of the text, a set of multiple choice and open questions is waiting for you.

Buona fortuna! *Good luck!*

🔊 IL LAVORO DEI MIEI SOGNI

Da bambina, non ho mai sognato di diventare un'astronauta, una ballerina, una cantante o una modella. Il mio sogno è sempre stato quello di diventare una chef.

Ho preparato dei piatti deliziosi con una piccola cucina di plastica, il regalo più bello che mi hanno fatto i miei genitori. Ho obbligato tutti i miei parenti a gustare i miei finti piatti e bevande, che loro hanno sempre finto di amare alla follia.

Quando sono andata alle scuole medie, il mio sogno non è mai cambiato. Ho iniziato ad aiutare mia mamma in cucina: ho preparato il mio primo vero dolce, un tiramisù! È stata un'esperienza bellissima che mi ha convinto ancora di più sul mio futuro.

Una volta arrivato il momento di scegliere la scuola superiore, ho deciso di frequentare l'alberghiero, una scuola professionale dove gli studenti imparano a cucinare, a servire in hotel e ristoranti, e molto altro ancora.

Ho studiato tantissimo perché sono sempre stata ambiziosa e ho voluto imparare il più possibile. Ho fatto i miei compiti fino a tarda notte per ottenere il massimo dei voti. A volte ho fallito, mi sono arrabbiata, ma poi ho capito che fa tutto parte del gioco.

Mi sono diplomata con il massimo dei voti e ho iniziato subito a lavorare in un ristorante come stagista. Mi è sembrato di vivere finalmente il sogno di una vita.

Ho fatto turni estenuanti, sono tornata a casa alle 5 della mattina, e i miei genitori mi hanno fatto molte domande: Sei sicura della tua scelta? Vuoi davvero vivere così?

Ma mi hanno sempre supportato, e io sono sempre stata determinata, ho continuato. Ho continuato per cominciare a mettere da parte i primi risparmi. Ho fatto molti sacrifici, ma non mi pento.

Dopo anni, ora posso dire che il mio sogno è realtà. Ho aperto un piccolo ristorante in centro città e ho quattro persone che lavorano con me. Vado a lavorare ogni giorno con il sorriso, lo stesso sorriso che ho avuto per anni da bambina.

ESERCIZI
EXERCISES

1) Quiz: scegli la risposta corretta. *Quiz: choose the right answer*

Il testo parla di un bambino. *The text is about a boy:*

- **Vero** *True*
- **Falso** *False*

Qual era il suo lavoro dei sogni? *What was his/her dream job?*

- **Ballerina** *dancer*
- **Cantante** *singer*
- **Cuoca** *cook*
- **Attrice** *actress*

Che scuola ha frequentato? *Which school did he/she attend?*

- **Liceo scientifico**
- **Alberghiero**
- **Liceo linguistico**
- **Nessuna scuola** *(none)*

Ha sempre ottenuto buoni voti. *He/she always got good grades:*

- **Vero** *True*
- **Falso** *False*

Dove ha iniziato a lavorare? *Where did he/she started working?:*

- **In un hotel** *in a hotel*
- **In un ristorante** *in a restaurant*
- **In una pizzeria** *in a pizzeria*

I suoi genitori erano dubbiosi *His/her parents had some doubts.*

- **Vero** *True*
- **Falso** *False*

Adesso ha un suo bar *Now he/she has his/her own café*

- **Vero** *True*
- **Falso** *False*

2) Rispondi alle seguenti domande. *Answer the following questions:*

Qual è il lavoro che hai sognato da bambino/a? Perché? *What was your dream job when you were a child? Why?*

_____

_____

_____

_____

Il tuo sogno è rimasto lo stesso per tutta la tua vita? Che lavoro fai oggi? *When you grew up was your dream job still the same? What is your job today?*

_____

_____

_____

_____

Traduzione
Translation

My dream job

When I was a child, I never dreamt about becoming an astronaut, a dancer, a singer or a model. My dream was to become a chef.

I prepared delicious meals with a small kitchen made of plastic, the best gift my parents ever gave me. I forced all my relatives to taste my fake meals and drinks that they always pretended to appreciate deeply.

When I went to middle school, my dream did not change. I started helping my mother in the kitchen and I prepared my first real dessert, a tiramisu! An amazing experience that convinced me even more about the future I wanted.

When I had to choose my new high school, I decided to attend the alberghiero, a professional school where students learn to cook, serve in hotels and restaurants, and much more.

I studied a lot as I have always been ambitious, and I wanted to learn as much as I could. I did my homework until late at night in order to get the best grades. Sometimes I failed, I got angry with myself, but then I learned that it was all part of the game.

I graduated with the highest grade, and I immediately started working in a restaurant as an intern. I felt like I was living the dream of a lifetime.

I have done exhausting shifts; I came back home at 5 a.m. and my parents used to ask me many questions. Are you sure about your choice? Do you really want to live this way?

But they have always supported me; I have always been very determined, and I kept on working. I kept on working to start saving some money. I have made many sacrifices, but I do not regret it.

After many years, now I can say that my dream came true. I opened a small restaurant in the city center, and I have four people working with me. I go to work every day with a smile on my face, the same smile I had for years when I was a child.

PARTICIPI PASSATI IRREGOLARI
IRREGULAR PAST PARTICIPLE

Infinitive form	Past participle
Aprire *to open*	**Aperto** *opened*
Accendere *to switch on*	**Acceso** *switched on*
Bere *to drink*	**Bevuto** *drunk*
Chiedere *to ask*	**Chiesto** *asked*
Chiudere *to close*	**Chiuso** *closed*
Correre *to run*	**Corso** *run*
Decidere *to decide*	**Deciso** *decided*
Dire *to say/tell*	**Detto** *said/told*
Dividere *to divide*	**Diviso** *divided*
Essere *to be*	**Stato** *been*
Fare *to do/make*	**Fatto** *done/made*
Leggere *to read*	**Letto** *read*
Mettere *to put*	**Messo** *put*
Nascere *to be born*	**Nato/a** *born*
Perdere *to lose*	**Perso** *lost*
Piangere *to cry*	**Pianto** *cried*
Prendere *to take*	**Preso** *taken*
Ridere *to laugh*	**Riso** *laughed*
Rimanere *to stay*	**Rimasto** *stayed*
Rispondere *to answer*	**Risposto** *answered*
Scegliere *to choose*	**Scelto** *chosen*
Scendere *to get off*	**Sceso** *got off*
Scoprire *to find out*	**Scoperto** *found out*
Scrivere *to write*	**Scritto** *written*
Spegnere *to switch off*	**Spento** *switched off*
Spendere *to spend – money*	**Speso** *spent*
Succedere *to happen*	**Successo** *happened*
Togliere *to take off*	**Tolto** *taken off*
Tradurre *to translate*	**Tradotto** *translated*
Vedere *to see*	**Visto** *seen*
Venire *to come*	**Venuto** *come*
Vivere *to live*	**Vissuto** *lived*
Vincere *to win*	**Vinto** *won*

CONCLUSIONI
CONCLUSIONS

We have now come to the end of this journey into the Italian language. Obviously, there are still many things to say, and tons of new words to learn, but we really hope that this will be just the first step in your learning process.

Now it is your turn!

In order to keep on improving your Italian and feel more confident about it, here are a few suggestions:

1. Do not feel disappointed if you are not that fluent yet. Learning a new language takes **time** and, most importantly, a lot of **practice!** Don't lose your motivation and enjoy the challenges of the language. *Ce la puoi fare!* You can do it!

2. **Celebrate** every single accomplishment, no matter how small they are. Were you able to understand a whole video in Italian? Or maybe just a part of it? Did you pronounce a few sentences correctly? Did you remember some useful vocabulary? You should celebrate, then! *Festeggia!*

3. Use all the **resources** that you can find in order to improve your knowledge. Movies, podcasts, songs, TV series, everything is useful!

4. Take every opportunity you have to talk to someone in Italian. And **don't be afraid** of making mistakes. Mistakes are a normal – and very useful - part of the learning process.

5. *Divertiti!* **Have fun!**

ANSWER KEY

Section 1

Esercizi/Exercises I

1) 🔊 Quale lettera? *Which letter?*

Acca ➜ H	Esse ➜ S	Ci ➜ C
Zeta ➜ Z	Kappa ➜ K	A ➜ A
Emme ➜ M	Bi ➜ B	Vi ➜ V
Ti ➜ T	Doppia vu ➜ W	Erre ➜ R
Di ➜ D	I lunga ➜ J	Enne ➜ N
Effe ➜ F	Ics ➜ X	Ipsilon ➜ Y

2) Numeri e suoni. *Numbers and sounds*

4 = Quattro - 59 = Cinquantanove - 165 = Centosessantacinque - 9 = Nove

62 = Sessantadue - 15 = Quindici - 2 = Due - 116 = Centosedici

123 = Centoventitré - 90 =   Novanta - 37 = Trentasette - 99 = Novantanove

7 = Sette - 41 = Quarantuno - 77 = Settantasette - 172 = Centosettantadue

12 = Dodici - 55 = Cinquantacinque - 137 = Centotrentasette - 17 = Diciassette

102 = Centodue - 24 = Ventiquattro - 11 = Undici - 66 = Sessantasei

8 = Otto -149 = Centoquarantanove - 95 = Novantacinque - 34 = Trentaquattro

Esercizi/Exercises II

1) Femminile o Maschile? *Feminine –F or Masculine –M?*

Divano (couch) = M	Libro (book) = M
Sedia (chair) = F	Professore (professor) = M
La pilota (pilot) = F	Lampada (lamp) = F
Pino (pine tree) = M	Cane (dog) = M
Gelato (ice cream) = M	Lago di Como (Lake Como) = M
Il cantante (singer) = M	Cammello (camel) = M
Bicicletta (bike) = F	Palla (ball) = F
Musica (music) = F	Bicchiere (glass) = M
Pappagallo (parrot) = M	Madre (mother) = F
Scrittrice (writer) = F	Collo (neck) = M

2) Aggiungi la parola. *Write the feminine nouns in UPPER CASE and the masculine nouns in lower case in the right spaces. Use the dictionary for help.*

Feminine	Masculine
SEDIA	Telefono
SCRIVANIA	Computer
MATITA	Libro
PENNA	Foglio
AGENDA	
LAMPADA	

Esercizi/Exercises III

1) Trova il plurale. *Find the plural.*

Albergo (hotel) = Alberghi

Asparago (asparagus) = Asparagi

Zaino (backpack) =   Zaini

Ciliegia (cherry) = Ciliegie

Pera (pear) = Pere

Barca (boat) = Barche

Fotografia (picture) = Fotografie

Uovo (egg) = Uova

Cartello (sign) = Cartelli

Faro (lighthouse) = Fari

Cardiologo (cardiologist) = Cardiologi

Strega (witch) = Streghe

Insalata (salad) = Insalate

Libro (book) = Libri

2) Genere e Numero. *Gender and Number.*

Maschile, singolare	Maschile, plurale	Femminile, singolare	Femminile, plurale
Piatto	Letti	Finestra	Televisioni
Leone	Telefoni	Guida	Spazzole
Specchio	Fuochi	Scatola	Galline
Falco	Cappelli		Zuppe
Occhio			

3) Trova il singolare. *Find the singular.*

Lampade (lamps) = Lampada

Coltelli (knives) = Coltello

Psicologi (psychologists) = Psicologo

Giornali (newspapers) = Giornale

Tavoli (tables) = Tavolo

Cani (dogs) = Cane

Pulcini (chicks) = Pulcino

Laghi (lakes) = Lago

Orecchini (earrings) = Orecchino

Carte (papers) = Carta

Guanti (gloves) = Guanto

Coperte (blankets) = Coperta

Papere (ducks) = Papera

Pentole (pots) = Pentola

Porte (doors) = Porta

Navi (boats) = Nave

Mari (seas) = Mare

Costumi (costumes) = Costume

Esercizi/Exercises IV

1) Articoli indeterminativi. *Choose the right indefinite article.*

Un	Una	Uno	Un'
Gelato	Chiesa	Zaino	Ala
Gatto	Nave	Studente	Asse
Albergo	Candela	Specchio	Automobile
Istituto			
Capello			

2) Correggi gli errori. *Correct the mistakes.*

Le stivali sono belli (The boots are nice) = Gli stivali sono belli

Il ufficio è chiuso (The office is closed) = L'ufficio è chiuso

Mangia lo pasta (Eat the pasta) = Mangia la pasta

Gli bicchieri sono rotti (The glasses are broken) = I bicchieri sono rotti

I squalo è morto (The shark is dead) = Lo squalo è morto

I pollo è scappato (The chicken escaped) = Il pollo è scappato

Lo porte sono aperte (The doors are open) = Le porte sono aperte

3) Scegli l'articolo partitivo. *Pick the right partitive article.*

Devi comprare del pane.

Ho imparato delle canzoni.

Porta dei piatti.

Cucina della pasta.

Ho perso degli orecchini.

Ha bisogno di spazio per crescere.

Ho visto degli uccelli.

4) Dal Singolare al Plurale. *From Singular to Plural*

La zuppa (the soup) = Le zuppe

Il dolce (the sweet) = I dolci

Il leone (the lion) = I leoni

Il libro (the book) = I libri

La lingua (the tongue/language) = Le lingue

Lo stivale (the boot) = Gli stivali

La vita (the life) = Le vite

L'orso (the bear) = Gli orsi

Lo scudo (the shield) = Gli scudi

L'ape (the bee) = Le api

Section 2

Esercizi/Exercises I

1) Saluti. *Greetings*

- It is late at night, and you are going to sleep. What do you say to your uncle?

    d) Buonanotte

- After waking up, you walk to the café for an *espresso*. How do you greet the barista?

    b) Salve c) Buongiorno

- You have just finished having dinner with friends, and you are about to leave. How do you say goodbye to them?

    a) Ciao

- It is 3 p.m., and someone is knocking at your door. You open the door, and in front of you, there is an older person delivering your food. How do you greet him?

    d) Buon pomeriggio

- You are leaving a store, and you want to say goodbye to the shop assistant. What do you say?

    c) Arrivederci

- You are meeting your friend Paolo for lunch, and he introduces you to his 6-year-old son. What do you say when you first meet him?

    b) Ciao

- In a few minutes, you will have an interview for a new job. The Human Resource Manager is a woman around your age. How do you greet her?

    d) Salve

- You are breaking up with your girlfriend/boyfriend. The last line of your letter reads:

    d) Addio

2) Tu o Lei? *Which one would you pick? Underline the correct one*

Your best friend? Tu / A small child? Tu / A stranger at the bus stop? Lei / An older man? Lei / Your grandfather? Tu.

Esercizi/Exercises II

1) 🔊 **Pronomi Personali Soggetto.** *Subject Personal Pronouns*

Cara Alice,

Oggi sono andata al mare. <u>Io</u> non volevo andare, ma mia mamma ha insistito. <u>Lei</u> non è venuta, ma mia sorella era con me. <u>Noi</u> abbiamo preso un gelato e ci siamo divertite molto. <u>Tu</u> cosa hai fatto oggi?

Vorrei tanto vedere te e la tua famiglia, <u>voi</u> venite mai da queste parti?

Un caro saluto.

2) 🔊 **Pronomi Personali Oggetto.** *Object Personal Pronouns*

Caro Gino,

Sono molto contenta di aver<u>ti</u> visto l'altro giorno. Puoi aiutar<u>mi</u> con il mio progetto? <u>Ti</u> potrebbe interessare? Fam<u>mi</u> sapere se hai intenzione di venire a trovar<u>mi</u> ancora.

Consci i figli di Vittoria? Ieri <u>li</u> abbiamo visti al cinema.

Un abbraccio.

Esercizi/Exercises III

1) Verbo essere *to be*

Emma è una bambina di sette anni. / Loro sono felici per me. / Hai visto il giornale? Noi siamo in prima pagina. / Io non sono vecchia! / Il mio amico è in ritardo. / Tu sei molto gentile.

2) Verbo avere *to have*

Voi avete una pizza. / Io ho ho due gatti. / Marta ha 4 fratelli. / Noi abbiamo una macchina. / Loro hanno un appuntamento. / Lui ha un bicchiere.

3) Verbo avere/essere *to have/to be*

Giovanni è molto ricco. / Loro hanno molti soldi. / Il cane è fuori. / Tu hai dei compiti? / Loro sono giovani. / Io sono stanco. / La bicicletta è rotta. /

4) 🔊 **Essere o avere?** *To be or to have?*

Aurora ha gli occhiali. / La pecora è scappata. / Noi abbiamo festeggiato. / Lui è allegro. / Il panda ha mangiato. / Loro hanno finito. / Marco è uno studente. / Noi siamo stanchi.

Esercizi/Exercises IV

1) Completa le frasi. *Complete the sentences by conjugating the verb in the present tense.*

Parte - mangio – leggono – abbaiano – corriamo – accende – cucini – dorme – studiate – compro.

2) Coniuga i verbi. *Conjugate the following verbs at the present tense.*

Io	Guardo	Cado	Parto
Tu	Guardi	Cadi	Parti
Lui/Lei	Guarda	Cade	Parte
Noi	Guardiamo	Cadiamo	Partiamo
Voi	Guardate	Cadete	Partite
Loro	Guardano	Cadono	Partono

Esercizi/Exercises V

1) Completa le frasi. *Complete the sentences by conjugating the verb in the present tense.*

Esce – vado – sai – fanno – saliamo - potete

2) Scegli il verbo. *Pick the correct verb from those listed below to complete the paragraph.*

Arianna tutte le mattine fa colazione e poi esce di casa e va all'università. Quando non ha lezione, Arianna esce con le amiche. Loro vanno al museo o fanno una corsa. Arianna dice che correre fa bene e la rilassa. Questa sera Arianna vuole vedere un film con sua mamma.

Esercizi/Exercises VI

1) Scegli la parola giusta. *Fill in the blanks with the appropriate word.*

Ciao – stai

bene

sto

chiamo

signora – sta

Esercizi/Exercises VII

1) Accorda l'aggettivo. *Fill in the blanks by translating the adjective in the parenthesis.*

Magri – rossi – timidi – verdi – creativa – basso – generosi – biondi – cattiva

2) Scegli l'aggettivo. *Find the Italian adjective that fits the description.*

Timida – basso – creative – cattivo – brutta – bella – impaziente – attraente – alta

Esercizi/Exercises VIII

1) Unisci testo e immagine. *Connect the picture with the correct profession.*

A-7 / B-3 / C-12 / D-9 / E-11 / F-2 / G-1 / H-10 / I-8 / L-5 / M-6 / N-4

2) Che lavoro fanno? *What is their job?*

Cameriere – Cameriera / Maestro – Maestra / Impiegato – Impiegata / Giornalista – Giornalista / Direttore – Direttrice / Architetto – Architetto / Pilota – Pilota / Dentista – Dentista / Ingegnere – Ingegnere / Dottore – Dottoressa / Farmacista – Farmacista.

3) Dove lavorano? *Where do they work?*

Ristorante: cameriere – cuoco / Scuola: insegnante / Fabbrica: operaio / Ufficio: impiegato – segretario – manager / Negozio: commesso / Ospedale: dottore – infermiere / Studio: ingegnere – avvocato – architetto – informatico / Teatro: attrice – regista.

Esercizi/Exercises IX

1) Completa le frasi. *Complete the following sentences with the correct prepositions.*

La lezione finisce alle 11. / Vado a Milano in aereo. / Il nonno porta i bambini al parco. / Sono in macchina, arrivo tra 5 minuti. / Il film è al cinema.

2) 🔊 Ascolta l'audio. *Listen to the audio file and fill in the blanks with the right preposition.*

(Loro) vanno a teatro domani sera. / Francesco va dal dottore. / Oggi voglio andare a letto presto. / Pietro incontra gli amici al bar. / Ogni mattina Nicoletta prende il caffè con me. / Luciana è in Svizzera. / Vieni a trovarmi a Torino? / Vado all'università. / Prendo la matita per disegnare. / Vado al mercato.

Esercizi/Exercises X

1) Da dove vieni? *Write the two options to express someone's origins using the subject pronouns in brackets.*

Tu sei tedesco/a - vieni dalla Germania; noi siamo inglesi - veniamo dall'Inghilterra; lui è francese - viene dalla Francia; lei è americana - lei viene dagli Stati Uniti; siete spagnole - venite dalla Spagna; sono cinese - vengo dalla Cina.

Esercizi/Exercises XI

1) Aggiungi il colore. *Add the right form of the color according to the noun that follows.*

rosa – nere – i pantaloni grigi scuri – verde – rosso – nera e bianca – arancioni, gialli e blu – viola.

2) Di che colore è....? *What color is....?*

Il mio zaino è *nero* – Oggi il cielo è *blu chiaro* – I vestiti che porto sono *rossi e bianchi* – La mia maglietta preferita è *verde scuro*.

Esercizi/Exercises XII

1) Aggiungi l'aggettivo possessivo. *Add the right form of article and possessive adjective according to the noun that follows.*

Il loro – le nostre – il suo – la tua – i suoi – il mio – la tua – i nostri – il suo – i miei – la loro.

2) Con o senza l'articolo? *With or without the article?*

I suoi figli – il mio cane – nostro padre – i vostri vestiti – la tua borsa – i miei cugini – suo cugino

3) Trova l'errore. Find the mistake. *Read the following sentences and correct the mistakes - if any.*

I nostri letti - La vostra cucina - La sua pazienza - Il tuo computer - La mia vicina - Le tue vacanze - La sua emergenza - Le loro storie - Vostro fratello.

Esercizi/Exercises XIII

1) Scriviamo! *Write a short text about your family using the verb to have.*

This exercise concerns the reader's ability to describe his or her family.

2) 🔊 **Ascolta l'audio.** *Listen to the audio file and fill in the blanks with the right word.*

Ciao! Mi chiamo Laura e questa è la mia famiglia. Amo molto i miei genitori, papà Paolo e mamma Lucia, e anche mia nonna Carla, che lavorava come cuoca da giovane. Ho un fratello minore, Luca, che studia al liceo, e una sorella maggiore, Giulia, che lavora come ingegnere. Poi ci sono io! Studio matematica all'università e vorrei diventare una professoressa. La mia famiglia è tutto per me!

3) Con o senza l'articolo? *Add the right possessive adjective and article—when present—in front of the family members.*

i tuoi – la – il – i suoi – la – le loro – i miei – le sue

Section 3

Esercizi/Exercises I

1) Che ore sono? *Write the time in Italian.*

Sono le quattro e mezzo – sono le tre/quindici e un quarto – sono le sei/diciotto meno un quarto – sono le due e cinquanta/sono le tre meno dieci – è mezzanotte – sono le sette/diciannove e venti – sono le sei (in punto) – sono le otto e mezzo – sono le quattro/sedici e dieci – è mezzogiorno – sono le due/quattordici meno cinque.

2) Completa il dialogo. *Complete the dialogue.*

Ciao Sara! – sono – sono le dieci e mezzo – prego, ciao!

3) Disegniamo! *Draw the hands of the clock.*

5:25 - 4:15 p.m. - 12:45 - 7:30 p.m. - 7:40

Esercizi/Exercises II

1) Rispondi alle domande. *Answer the question with a date, a day of the week or a month.*

Examples of possible answers: Il 21 settembre 2000 - Il 3 agosto - Mercoledì e venerdì - Luglio e agosto, o a febbraio

2) Scrivi le date. *Write the following dates in Italian - article included.*

L'uno febbraio – L'otto dicembre – Il 25 settembre – l'11 maggio – Il 13 gennaio – Il 6 marzo

Esercizi/Exercises III

1) Traduzione. *Translation. Please translate the following sentences into Italian.*

Prendo il treno alle diciotto/sei – Un biglietto sola andata, per favore – Il suo volo parte alle quattro e mezzo – Ho il mio passaporto e due biglietti – Vanno in bici – Siamo in ritardo! – Parte con la macchina/con l'auto – Torno a casa alle ventidue/dieci.

2) 🔊 Ascolta l'audio. *Listen to the audio file and fill in the blanks with the right word.*

Quando viaggio, mi piace scoprire nuove città e culture. Vado spesso in aereo perché è il mezzo di trasporto più veloce e non è quasi mai in ritardo. Porto con me solo il bagaglio a mano.
Prendo sempre i miei biglietti online.

Esercizi/Exercises IV

1) Completa la domanda. *Add the right WH question.*

Chi ha preso la macchina? - Che cosa hai fatto ieri? - Perché va a letto presto? - Quanti cuscini ci sono sul divano? - Come stai? - Quante magliette hanno comprato? - Quando finisci di lavorare? - Quanto olio d'oliva devo mettere?

2) Traduci le domande. *Translate the questions to the following answers.*

Quale è la sua casa? – Chi è la loro sorella? – Che cosa scrivi? – Quante macchine hai? – Dove è la mia valigia? – Perché ha la tua bici?

Esercizi/Exercises V

1) Coniuga il verbo. *Conjugate the modal verb.*

Il mio amico deve lavorare la domenica. - Vorrei un panino, grazie. - Mia sorella vuole studiare il cinese. - Posso chiedere la tua opinione? - Franco e Antonella vorrebbero andare all'estero. - Puoi venire ad aiutarmi?

2) 🔊 Ascolta l'audio. *Listen to the audio file and fill in the blanks with the right word.*

Quando posso, mi piace andare al ristorante e provare dei piatti nuovi. Devo stare attento ai prezzi, però! Vorrei trovare dei buoni ristoranti senza dovere spendere troppo. Ho una prenotazione per lunedì sera alle 8. Vuoi venire con me?

Esercizi/Exercises VI

1) Scrivi un'email. *Write an email to a hotel in Rome to book a room.*

Example:

Buongiorno,

Mi chiamo Paolo Rossi e vorrei prenotare una camera per tre persone (due adulti e un bambino di 11 anni) per tre notti, dal 14 giugno al 17. Vorremo la colazione inclusa. L'hotel ha un parcheggio? Possiamo fare il check out a mezzogiorno?

Cordiali saluti,

Paolo Rossi

Esercizi/Exercises VII

1) 🔊 Ascolta l'audio. *Listen to the audio file and fill in the blanks with the right words/sentences.*

Pronto?

Buongiorno! Vorrei un tavolo per domenica a pranzo. Avete posto?

Buongiorno signora. Sì, abbiamo posto. Per quante persone?

Siamo in cinque. È possibile?

Certamente. A che ora?

Alle 13.

Benissimo, a domenica!

A domenica, arrivederci!

Esercizi/Exercises VIII

1) Traduzione. *Translate the following sentences into Italian.*

Vorrei una pizza e una birra, per favore – Posso pagare in contanti? – Vorremmo due bicchieri di vino, per favore – Vorrei un piatto di pasta con il salmone e lei vorrebbe un'insalatona con il tonno.

2) 🔊 Ascolta l'audio. *Listen to the audio file and fill in the blanks with the right words/sentences.*

Buongiorno! Siete pronti per ordinare?

Sì! Prendiamo prosciutto e melone come antipasto e due piatti di pasta alle vongole.

Perfetto. Cosa vi porto da bere?

Una bottiglia d'acqua naturale, grazie.

Benissimo. A tra poco.

Esercizi/Exercises IX

1) Aggiungi l'articolo. *Add the right article in front of the food. Tip: pay attention to the word ending!*

il maiale – i polli – la spigola – le patate – il tonno – i cavoli – i carciofi– l'insalata – il peperone

2) Ti piace o non ti piace? *Add the foods that you like (mi piace) and do not like (non mi piace) in the following table.*

The exercise focuses on the reader's personal tastes regarding the different foods studied so far.

Esercizi/Exercises X

1) Traduzione. *Translate the following verbs into Italian.*

Mi lavo – ci incontriamo – si sono innamorati – ti alzi – si veste – si sposano – mi chiamo Marco

3) Coniuga il verbo. *Write the conjugation of the reflexive verbs of the example above.*

Svegliarsi	Farsi	Prepararsi
mi sveglio	mi faccio	mi preparo
ti svegli	ti fai	ti prepari
si sveglia	si fa	si prepara
ci svegliamo	ci facciamo	ci prepariamo
vi svegliate	vi fate	vi preparate
si svegliano	si fanno	si preparano

Esercizi/Exercises XI

1) Rispondi alle domande. *Answer the following questions.*

Posta – piscina – cinema – comune – museo – parco

2) 🔊 Ascolta l'audio. *Listen to the audio file and fill in the blanks with the right words.*

Abito in una piccola città vicino Milano. Non ci sono molti negozi, ma abbiamo una piscina e un cinema abbastanza grande. Il mio posto preferito è il museo locale, in cui è possibile ammirare molte statue antiche. Ci sono anche tre scuole e un parco enorme che mi piace molto.

Esercizi/Exercises XII

1) Dov'è...? *Look at the map and answer the following questions.*

Il palazzetto dello sport è accanto alla stazione degli autobus – Piazza Fontana è davanti alla fontana – La stazione dei treni è tra via della Repubblica e viale della Stazione – I giardini pubblici sono davanti alla scuola.

2) Osserva la cartina. *Look at the map and answer the following questions, giving the right directions or asking for the right ones.*

Deve andare a sinistra, poi girare a sinistra e andare sempre dritto – Mi scusi, dov'è la stazione degli autobus? – Deve andare a destra e poi girare a destra, Corso Garibaldi, e andare sempre dritto – Deve andare a destra, poi girare a sinistra, Via Monti, e andare dritto. La libreria è sulla destra.

Esercizi/Exercises XIII

1) Il meteo. *Look at the weather forecast and describe the weather in Italy.*

Example: Al nord è soleggiato, al sud c'è la tempesta e piove, ad est piove ed è nuvoloso. Ad ovest c'è il sole.

2) Che tempo fa oggi? *What is the weather like today in your city? Describe it in Italian using the vocabulary you have just learned.*

This exercise involves a description of the weather conditions related to the reader's country.

Esercizi/Exercises XIV

1) Chiedi il prezzo. *Ask for the price of the following items and answer the question according to the price shown.*

Quanto costa la pizza? La pizza costa sette euro – Quanto costa la gonna? La gonna costa quindici euro – Quanto costano i calzini? I calzini costano tre euro e cinquanta.

2) 🔊 Ascolta l'audio. *Listen to the audio file and fill in the blanks with the right words.*

Buongiorno, come posso aiutarla?

Salve, quanto costa questo orologio?

Cinquanta euro.

Lo trovo un po' costoso, ma lo prendo comunque.

Perfetto, possiamo andare alla cassa. Mi segua.

Section 4

Esercizi/Exercises I

1) Rispondi alle domande. *Answer the following questions.*

The exercise should be filled out according to the sport played by the reader.

2) Giocare o fare? *Which verb(s) can you use to talk about the following sports? Put an X in the table below.*

Giocare a / fare calcio

Giocare a / fare golf

Fare equitazione

Giocare a / fare pallavolo

Fare danza

Fare ciclismo

Giocare a / fare pallamano

Fare nuoto

Esercizi/Exercises II

1) Rispondi alle domande. *Answer the following questions:*

The answers are entirely personal and based on the reader's hobbies.

Example:

- Mi piace *dipingere*

- Nel fine settimana pi piace *fare trekking*

- Al mio migliore amico piace *andare al cinema*

2) Metti una X. *Put an X in the table below to indicate whether you like those hobbies (mi piace) or not (non mi piace).*

This exercise relies on the reader's preferences.

Esercizi/Exercises III

1) Traduzione. *Translate the following sentences into Italian.*

Giulio è più alto di mio cugino – Il basket è meno faticoso della pallavolo – I libri sono più interessanti dei videogiochi – Mia sorella è tanto divertente quanto i suoi amici – Il golf è meno dinamico della pallamano.

2) Il comparativo. *Change the sentence—and the comparative—so that it has the same meaning.*

La pianta è meno bella del fiore – I cani sono meno furbi dei gatti – La lezione di matematica è più noiosa di quella di storia – Il libro è più colorato del quaderno.

Esercizi/Exercises IV

1) Superlativo Relativo (SR) or Superlativo Assoluto (SA)? *Write the abbreviation next to the following sentences.*

SR – SA – SR – SA – SR

2) Scrivi la frase. *Write the following sentences with the right superlativo relativo or superlativo assoluto.*

La tartaruga è la più lenta degli animali – I miei zii sono gentilissimi – Le stelle sono grandissime – Voi siete i più alti della famiglia.

Esercizi/Exercises V

1) Collega gli avverbi. *Link the adverb of frequency in English with the corresponding Italian one.*

Never - Mai

Sometimes - A volte

Often - Spesso

Always - Sempre

Rarely - Raramente

Usually - Solitamente

2) Le tue abitudini. *In Italian, write some activities that you always – sometimes – often – rarely – usually do.*

This exercise is based on the reader's activities.

Esercizi/Exercises VI

1) Scrivi un messaggio. *Write a text to your friend Marco.*

The exercise involves the ability to make an appointment and plan a meeting with a friend based on the information learned so far.

2) Scrivi un'email. *Write an email to your professor at the university.*

The exercise involves the ability to write a formal email to make an appointment with a professor using all the information learned so far.

Section 5

Esercizi/Exercises I

1) *Essere o avere?* *To be (essere) or to have (avere) as the auxiliary verb? Put an X in the table below.*

Essere: andare-partire-succedere-vestirsi-cadere

Avere: prendere-accendere-credere-vedere

2) Traduzione. *Translate the following verbs into Italian. Please note that there may be some irregular past participles.*

Sei andato/a – sono stato/a – hanno avuto – ha preso – abbiamo sperato – avete creato – è partito – ho provato.

3) 🔊 Ascolta l'audio. *Listen to the audio file and fill in the blanks with the right words.*

Ieri sono andato al cinema con i miei amici e abbiamo visto un film molto divertente. Abbiamo preso dei popcorn e ci siamo seduti davanti allo schermo. Alla fine del film, siamo usciti per comprare un panino. Abbiamo mangiato alle 22, sono morto di fame! Poi sono tornato a casa.

Esercizi/Exercises II

1) E la tua scuola? *How is the school system in your country? What are the main pros and cons? Write a short text in Italian.*

This exercise involves the free production of a text based on the school system in the reader's country.

2) 🔊 Ascolta l'audio. *Listen to the audio file and fill in the blanks with the right words.*

Ho frequentato il Liceo linguistico nella mia città. Ho scelto quella scuola perché sono sempre stato appassionato alle lingue straniere. Ho studiato inglese e russo, ma la mia materia preferita era letteratura perché amo leggere. Ho sempre preso buoni voti e i miei genitori sono stati fieri di me quando ho preso il diploma.

Extra: Reading Comprehension

Esercizi/Exercises

1) Quiz: scegli la risposta corretta *Quiz: choose the right answer*

Falso - cuoca - alberghiero - falso - in un ristorante - vero - falso

2) Rispondi alle seguenti domande: *Answer the following questions*

This exercise requires answers based on the reader's experiences.

MORE BOOKS BY LINGO MASTERY

We are not done teaching you Italian until you're fluent!

Here are some other titles you might find useful in your journey of mastering Italian:

- *Italian Short Stories for Beginners*
- *Intermediate Italian Short Stories*
- *2000 Most Common Italian Words in Context*
- *Conversational Italian Dialogues*

But we got many more!

Check out all of our titles at **www.LingoMastery.com/italian**